IMPLEMENTING STRATEGY

IMPLEMENTING STRATEGY
Making Strategy Happen

The Staff of
MANAGEMENT ANALYSIS CENTER, INC.
Edited by
Paul J. Stonich

BALLINGER PUBLISHING COMPANY
Cambridge, Massachusetts
A Subsidiary of Harper & Row, Publishers, Inc.

International Standard Book Number: 0-88410-904-6

Library of Congress Catalog Card Number: 82-1667

Printed in the United States of America

Library of Congress Cataloging in Publication Data

Main entry under title:

Implementing strategy.

  Bibliography: p.
  Includes index.
  1. Organizational effectiveness. 2. Management. 3. Planning.
I. Stonich, Paul J. II. Management Analysis Center.
HD58.9.I46   658.4′012   82-1667
ISBN 0-88410-904-6   AACR2

Portions of Chapter 2 appeared as "Matching Corporate Culture and Business Strategy," by Howard M. Schwartz and Stanley M. Davis, in *Organizational Dynamics* (Summer 1981). These portions are © by AMACOM, a division of the American Management Association, and used by permission. All rights reserved. Mr. Schwartz is a MAC vice president; Dr. Davis is Professor of Organization Behavior at Boston University and a member of the MAC Board of Directors.

  Chapter 6 contains material originally appearing in "Strategic Funds Programming: The Missing Link in Corporate Planning," by Paul J. Stonich and Carlos E. Zaragoza, in *Managerial Planning* (September/October 1980). © 1980 by the Planning Executives Institute. Used by permission. Both Mr. Stonich and Mr. Zaragoza are MAC senior vice presidents.

CONTENTS

LIST OF EXHIBITS

FOREWORD

E. Kirby Warren, Columbia University

From the mid-1960s through the early 1970s, formulating strategy was often viewed as the key to success. Increasingly sophisticated techniques were offered to allow complex organizations to build strategies for the future. But far too many organizations separated strategy formulation from strategy implementation, and by the mid-1970s, many such organizations were finding these complicated strategies difficult to implement effectively. As a result, attention shifted to techniques for strategy implementation.

As a researcher and consultant on corporate planning systems for the past 23 years, I have been hoping for some time to see a book like this, which recognizes that questions of implementation must be answered *during* the formulation process, not later when it may be too late. In a positive, step-by-step manner, the authors get at the key to effective planning—*linking planning to action programs.* It is only through such linkages that organizations can develop strategies that are likely to result in effective implementation.

This is a thoughtful, conceptually sound treatment. Most of all, it is a practical guide to implementation. It considers all the central elements of strategy implementation—organization structure, human resources, corporate culture, and management processes—that must be tied to decisions on strategic direction. By posing questions and providing guides to resolving them, this book will help executives to take charge of the future for their organizations.

PREFACE

Over the past several years, the consultants of Management Analysis Center who contributed to this book have worked with hundreds of companies to help them implement their strategies. Some concentrated on specific areas, which could be categorized as strategy formulation, organization structure, human resources, corporate culture, and management process. As time passed and experience deepened, however, it became increasingly apparent that these areas are closely related, and that the common theme binding them together is implementing strategy.

A decision was made in the late 1970s to position Management Analysis Center's practice explicitly in the context of implementing strategy. As we became more focused in our practice, the consistent approach to implementing strategy presented in this book was developed and refined.

We began collecting material for this work in early 1980, and its major concepts were still evolving toward synthesis. As an established and rapidly growing management consulting firm, we initially intended to capture and communicate our experiences and broad outlook for internal use. We soon realized that the information might be of interest to a wider audience, and this view was shared by Carol Franco and Mike Connolly at Ballinger Publishing Company. We appreciate their confidence, help, and patience.

The list of contributors is long. All active contributors are full-time professional members of Management Analysis Center based in five offices in the United States, one in Latin America, and two in Europe. We also relied on published and unpublished research done by many of our 200 affiliated business school professors, and others, as noted in the Selected References that follow each chapter and in the Bibliography.

The hundreds of clients with whom Management Analysis Center has worked to implement strategy provided the experiences upon which much of this book is based. We wish to acknowledge this vital contribution from our clients.

Many people reviewed our manuscript and made suggestions for improvement. The insights of Professors Stanley M. Davis, E. Kirby Warren, Richard F. Vancil, and other faculty associated with Management Analysis Center were especially valuable.

Our internal editor, Sid Seamans, worked tirelessly to help us integrate, rewrite, and polish material. Joy Hebert provided editorial assistance on earlier drafts. The task of typing the many iterations of the manuscript was ably done by MAC's clerical staff.

Although all members of Management Analysis Center's professional staff provided assistance with the book, either through sharing experiences or reviewing the manuscript, the following members of the firm were its principal contributors:

Anne Benedict	David L. Jaffe
Lawrence A. Bennigson	James N. Kelly
Michael G. Bier	Alan R. Minoff
Michael L. Blyth	Charles H. Roush, Jr.
Bruce S. Buchowicz	Howard M. Schwartz
J. Martin Dalgleish	Donald E. Shay, Jr.
Arthur J. Daltas	Paul J. Stonich
Anne B. Evans	Howard P. Weil
Robert N. Gogel	Susan G. Wernecke
William T. Gregor	Carlos E. Zaragoza

Robert N. Gogel deserves special thanks. Bob helped draft several iterations of the manuscript and provided valuable conceptual support.

Any collective work such as this is bound to have omissions and imperfections, despite the best advice, and I take responsibility for any that have occurred.

Paul J. Stonich
Northbrook
February 1982

INTRODUCTION

Implementing strategy is not a new concept in business literature or in practice. Usually, however, its role has been placed in a secondary position to strategy formulation. The philosophy was that if the formulation effort was sound, implementation would follow automatically. As a result, many managers who saw strategy formulation as the cornerstone of their companies' success are now wondering why their elaborate strategies did not work as planned.

Comments from a number of chief executives,* gathered in a recent survey, reflect the need for a more comprehensive and integrated way to view the complex task of implementing strategy:

- "I believe you when you say the implementation aspects are important, but first I need to be sure that the strategies we develop are analytically based, practical, and make sense for us."
- "OK, you've convinced me that we need to change our strategic direction. But how will I ever convince my people to value innovation and entrepreneurship when, for twenty-five years, tradition, loyalty, and past success stories have dominated our product-development effort?"

*Because of the confidential nature of most of Management Analysis Center's client assignments, client companies and their staffs have not been named in this book. Circumstances of some cases have been changed to ensure confidentiality; where specific companies are named, the situations are general public knowledge.

- "The company has reorganized again—it's an annual event, almost like planning and budgeting. It's funny, though. Senior management keeps moving the boxes on the organization chart around, and still things stay the same."
- "Putting people in the right jobs at the right time without disrupting the organization is tough. We always seem to have the right people for last year's strategy."
- "Oh, yes, our company has a long-range planning process—a process full of paperwork, review sessions, more review sessions and, finally, approval. But approval often comes just in time to begin the process all over again."
- "We spend a lot of time formulating strategy, but we can never seem to get the right amount of money behind the high-priority strategies."
- "Around here, budgeting has become a mechanical activity. We use last year's budget as a base for preparing next year's budget, and add some fudge factor for contingencies. The problem really comes, though, when managers keep another budget that reflects their true intentions for the year."
- "Even though we are paid based on current performance, I still try to do what's best for the division over the long haul. But it's hard to ignore the impact on my paycheck."

The shared theme that emerges from these comments is that something is not working. And in each instance, that "something" is a narrow view of one element of strategy implementation, which results in a mismatch and conflict with the others. To deal with any one element without considering the others is to invite failure.

Clearly, identifying attractive opportunities and setting the right strategic direction—whether at the corporate or division level—do not, by themselves, guarantee success. As the methods used to formulate strategy become more sophisticated, and as the resulting strategies themselves become more precise and fine-tuned, corporate managers need to devote increasing attention to questions of execution.

Over the past decade, the crucial importance of execution has become even more apparent. It has been demonstrated repeatedly that successful performance occurs when an appropriate strategy is implemented through the effective rationalization of the basic elements that make up and drive an organization. In this book, we define these elements as strategy formulation, organization structure, human resources, management processes, and corporate culture. Success—

achievement of strategic objectives—is brought about through a complex interaction of strategy and all these elements.

Both formulation and implementation are, of course, major factors for successful strategic management. It is important at the outset, however, to recognize the essential difference between strategy formulation and implementation:

> Strategy formulation is deciding *where* your company is today and *where* your company should be tomorrow.

In contrast:

> Implementation is deciding *how* to get your company from where it is today to where it should be tomorrow.

Experience in assisting businesses of all sizes has produced convincing evidence that attacking a problem in one element of a company's activities can have far-reaching ramifications for the other elements. An organization will move most effectively toward its declared objectives when, and only when, all of its complex elements are synchronized. We frequently refer to this synchronization concept as "fit."

Each of the five elements—strategy formulation, culture, organization structure, human resources, and management processes—can be positioned as a strategic weapon. These weapons can, for instance, be used to erect barriers to entry or to enter new markets or businesses with competitive advantages. In a given circumstance, it may be appropriate to emphasize change in one specific element. However, the impact a change in one area has on the other elements should be borne in mind so that the integral "fit" among the elements is maintained.

Effectively implementing strategy thus requires a constant effort to match and fit together the basic elements that drive the organization. To gain a clearer perspective on these elements, we utilize the model shown in Exhibit I-1. While models are by nature nearly always oversimplified, this one is useful in showing the concerted interactions and the iterative process that must occur for an organization to succeed in today's business environment. It is also the unifying thread that ties this book together.

Exhibit I-1.   Implementing Strategy: The Model.

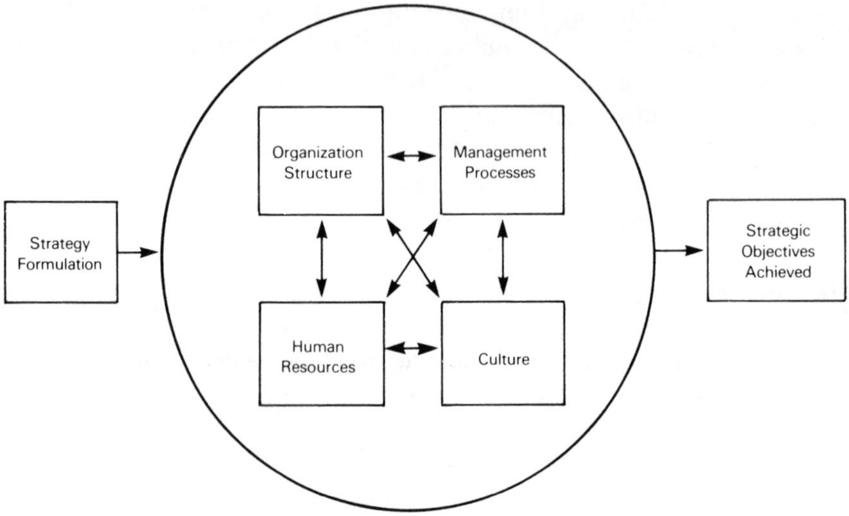

Chapter 1 deals with the first element in the model—strategy formulation. The methods available and choices to be made by managers in formulating strategy are numerous, but steps common to many of these methods include objective-setting, business definition, economic analysis, competitor analysis, market and company growth analysis, and resource allocation. But, as the model implies (and, indeed, as will be repeated time and again in this book), this external focus of strategy formulation must be balanced by assessments of internal capabilities— the organization's structure, human resources, management processes, and culture—in order to implement strategy effectively.

The process by which a strategy is formulated is, therefore, extremely important to the strategy's success. The appropriate process involves not only developing the "right" economic answer, but also ensuring that it can be implemented within the particular company.

Chapter 2 discusses culture. All organizations have cultures that delineate, in an unofficial and usually unspoken way, the "rules of the game." It is how things are really done. Recognizing the ramifications of the firm's culture is especially critical when implementing strategy because, in many respects, culture—more than any other element—dictates what can and will be done. Knowing how to assess the cultural risks inherent in a chosen strategy is a necessary skill for the effective manager of strategy.

Chapter 3 moves into the organization area of our model and examines the importance of the organization's structure. Broadly speaking, structure is the formal authority hierarchy that delineates the various roles, responsibilities, and reporting relationships within the firm. As discussed in Chapter 3, attempting to implement a desirable strategy can sometimes be constrained by the structure in place—that is, there may be a poor fit between the strategy and the structure. When this occurs, managers must investigate alternative structuring possibilities that will drive the chosen strategy, and in some cases the strategy may have to be refocused to fit the existing structure.

Human resources—the organization's people, their skills, experience, ability, and style—is the part of the model covered in Chapter 4. Very clearly, attempting to implement a strategy without people with the requisite skills, attitude, and training will lead to disaster. Again, managers must make difficult choices among altering the strategy to fit the available human resources, developing the skills of current people, or hiring the new people needed to bring the strategy to fruition.

Chapters 5 through 8 are concerned with the management process elements of the model. Management processes—planning, programming, budgeting, and rewarding—make up the vital "nervous system" that directs and sends signals throughout an organization and stimulates its movement toward the chosen objectives.

To begin, Chapter 5 covers the planning process. Planning is different from strategy formulation, in that it provides a "snapshot" of the firm's activities at a predetermined time, and its principal function is communication and consensus-building within the company. Strategy formulation, on the other hand, provides a detailed "motion picture" view of the firm over an extended period of time. Many decisions must be made about planning, including the amount of time to devote to strategic issues, the frequency with which to review business strategy, and the depth of management involvement in the planning process.

The process of converting strategic intentions into actions requires multiyear programming of capital and strategic expenses. As Chapter 6 makes clear, how to design and manage the programming process is a central issue. Decisions must be made about which expenditures should be programmed, how many years need to be considered, and which managers should be included in the programming effort.

Strategy is implemented through day-to-day activities that must be planned and controlled. Most companies use operating and capital budgeting techniques and understand their importance. But budgeting, the subject of Chapter 7, can often extend usefully beyond its traditional role by examining expenditures to ensure their utility and fit with basic strategy. If a company has large discretionary expenses and wide fluctuations in operating levels, for example, it may find that an emphasis on improving the traditional overhead budgeting process will produce substantial benefits.

Chapter 8 shows how measurement and reward systems reinforce chosen strategies and the other management processes. Performance measurement systems are most effective when they match the organization's structure and strategy. Tying compensation to long-term objectives and programs as well as to short-term profitability is a critical implementation step for strategic change. Choices in designing reward systems depend on the clarity and importance of long-term objectives and programs, as well as on the organization's ability to make qualitative judgments required by a long-term reward system.

Finally, Chapter 9 synthesizes and summarizes the elements of our model, none of which, of course, is actually discrete. All of the complex elements and actions required to move an organization toward its objectives must be raised to the conscious level, clearly understood and, as much as possible, made to work in unison. A strategic diagnosis is one way to evaluate the fit among them all, and can help an organization move more surely toward success.

1 STRATEGY FORMULATION

I believe you when you say the implementation aspects are important, but first I need to be sure that the strategies we develop are analytically based, practical, and make sense for us.—CEO of a Fortune 500 company.

Intensive strategy formulation for each strategic business unit (SBU) in a corporation should take place as the need arises. This is not a routine, annual process and is outside of the normal procedures undertaken each year to confirm strategic direction and allocate resources. The regular annual planning process is described in Chapter 5.

Following the logic of our model (see Exhibit 1–1), this chapter deals with the process and analysis to be used in intensive, irregular strategy formulation procedures. Practical and organizational issues are raised that need to be considered by managers and planners to ensure that the results of the process can, in fact, be implemented. This chapter is not meant to be a "how-to" treatment, but instead paints in broad strokes the concepts and issues involved in SBU strategy formulation. Central questions to consider include:

What are the major process impediments to developing a sound and practical strategy?

In what ways should line and staff managers participate in the strategy formulation process?

What factors should be considered in formulating strategy?

What analytical tools should be used in formulating strategy?

1

Exhibit 1–1.   Implementing Strategy: Strategy Formulation.

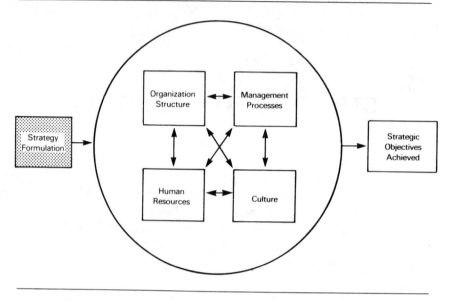

EVALUATING THE STRATEGY FORMULATION PROCESS

A successful strategy is: (a) analytical and fact-based; and (b) implementation- and consensus-oriented. The strategy formulation process therefore needs to emphasize these two critical dimensions.

It is possible to view these two dimensions as shown in the Exhibit 1–2 matrix. The vertical axis measures the degree to which the process is analytical and fact-based; the horizontal axis measures the degree to which the process is oriented toward consensus and implementation. Based on their current process of strategy formulation, companies can be positioned in one of the four quadrants—All Form/No Substance; Business-as-Usual; Ivory Tower; or the Winning Combination. Each position is described below.

All Form/No Substance

When strategic business unit (SBU) managers know that a strategy must be prepared for top management, but do not consider it impor-

Exhibit 1-2.   Evaluating the Strategy Formulation Process.

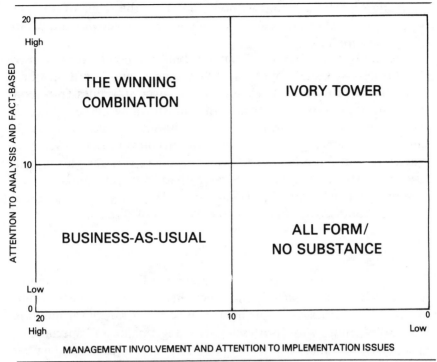

MANAGEMENT INVOLVEMENT AND ATTENTION TO IMPLEMENTATION ISSUES

tant enough to participate personally, they delegate it to staff assistants. Staff assistants develop the strategy by following instructions and by completing forms given to them by corporate staff. Although elaborate reports are prepared, they lack facts, analysis, and perspective. There is little objectivity, little senior management involvement, and no recognition of implementation issues. This method of formulation, which falls in the All-Form/No-Substance area in Exhibit 1-2, guarantees shallow strategies with little commitment to making them work. As might be expected, such strategies are not followed by top management and are therefore of little use.

Business-as-Usual

The lower left-hand box in Exhibit 1-2 depicts the Business-as-Usual form of strategy formulation. It does involve more managers than the All-Form/No-Substance approach, since a committee of SBU managers gets together and discusses the issues, but still without gathering outside facts and without stretching the scope of analysis beyond the usual business activities. Typically, objectivity and depth of analysis are lacking.

One company providing computerized information services typified the Business-as-Usual approach. Key managers and board members held annual retreats at a secluded resort over 100 miles from corporate headquarters. In three days of brainstorming, these top executives formulated the firm's strategy without calculating a single number or analyzing one piece of data. Needless to say, lower level managers found the resulting "seat-of-the-pants" strategies unrealistic and difficult to interpret. Strategy had to be reformulated by a committee of functional heads and key staff members over a period of three months, and then sold to the board of directors.

Ivory Tower

The upper right-hand corner of the matrix in Exhibit 1-2 represents the Ivory Tower approach. Management has little involvement, resulting in low awareness of implementation issues. Strategy formulation is often left entirely to "professional strategic planners" specializing in sophisticated analytical techniques. They are objective and gather facts to back up their conclusions, but while strategies formulated by such specialists can be theoretically correct, they frequently do not take into account implementation issues, such as the culture of the organization or the organization's overall ability to carry them out.

A diversified chemical company, for instance, did all of its strategic planning by the book. It hired outside consultants in strategy formulation to draft strategies and formulate plans. But the logically conceived strategies have never achieved their specified goals, mainly because key line managers had no idea how to execute the Ivory Tower plans.

The Winning Combination

The top left-hand corner of the matrix represents the Winning Combination. High levels of management involvement and awareness of implementation issues are combined with in-depth, objective analyses. A task force composed of SBU managers, internal corporate staff, and professional strategic planners formulates strategies. This approach takes more time and more effort than the other approaches, but it does the best job of formulating a realistic and implementable strategy.

A major paint manufacturer used this winning combination as a means to overcome its past commitment to functional, rather than corporate, strategies. Previously, management had relied on intuition instead of facts, and its style of supervision was often characterized by benign neglect. By setting up a representative task force, the company was able to refocus its strategy based on sound factual analysis, and to achieve consensus on its goals and objectives. The emphasis was not only on the theoretically correct strategy, but on one that the management team knew how to implement. The elements of corporate culture, organization structure, human resources, and management process were viewed as strategic weapons that were used to implement the strategy.

There are four major points requiring careful consideration in repositioning the strategy formulation process from one of the three less-effective quadrants in Exhibit 1–2 to the Winning Combination area. First, the implementation requirements must be kept in mind when evaluating possible alternative strategies. Can enough of the needed human resources be marshaled to make the strategy work? How will existing planning, budgeting, and reward processes have to be modified in order to keep up with the new strategy's requirements? Will the new strategy require full or partial reorganization? Does the proposed strategy go against the grain of current organizational values and norms of behavior?

Second, the appropriate people must be involved in the strategy formulation process. Top management (both corporate and divisional) play two central roles: providing strategic guidance, and motivating others to use the process effectively. Corporate staff and professional strategic planners play a leading role in coordinating the entire process and ensuring that overall corporate goals are met. Key line managers from the divisions must also take an active part in formulating the strategies they will later implement. Their perspectives and commitment are critical to making the strategies work. Procedures, paperwork, and extraneous planning meetings should be kept to a minimum to discourage these busy managers from delegating strategy formulation activities to low-level subordinates.

Third, professional strategic planners from outside the SBU can be effective in counteracting business-as-usual tendencies. Professional planners can help line managers take a fresh look at their businesses and guide the analysis and selection of appropriate strategies.

Finally, enough time and training must be allowed to gather the relevant data and analyze it properly. Line/staff deficiencies in these activities can be countered by using outside expertise. Proper analysis is vital to choosing the most effective strategies.

EVALUATING THE STRATEGY FORMULATION PROCESS

One useful method for quickly evaluating how well an organization's strategy formulation process is working is to ask the questions posed below. Originally developed as a diagnostic tool, this questionnaire also illustrates the central factors involved in an effective strategy formulation process as discussed earlier. A careful reading of the questions provides a meaningful look at the major issues involved in the strategy formulation process.

Questionnaire Used to Evaluate the Strategy Formulation Process

Section I
These questions concern the manager-participation and implementation aspects of strategy formulation (the horizontal axis in Exhibit 1-2).

Does the organization's strategy formulation process explicitly include implementation aspects (such as required reorganizations, staffing changes, modifications to systems and policies)?

No. Strategy formulation does not consider these factors. □ –0

Somewhat. Some implicit consideration is given to potential major implementation problems. □ –1

Yes. A complete analysis is done to assess the impacts and feasibility of these factors with respect to strategy implementation. □ –2

Does the reward system (promotions, salary adjustments, bonuses, etc.) support strategy formulation?

No. Performance is measured the same across business units and is not linked to strategic objectives. □ –0

Somewhat. The same performance measures are used for
all units, but different targets are set for each unit.   □ –1

Yes. Performance measures are weighted differently for
different units to motivate desired behavior.   □ –2

Do the strategic plans emphasize practical actions?

No. Plans are often unrealistic and of little use.   □ –0

Somewhat. It varies by author and/or topic.   □ –1

Yes. Plans are clear and practical at all levels.   □ –2

How would most middle-level managers evaluate the strategy formulation process?

It is considered a waste of time by most middle-level
managers.   □ –0

The process is perceived by about half of all middle-level
managers as useful.   □ –1

The process is widely accepted as an integral and useful
part of every manager's responsibilities.   □ –2

Are the decisions made in the strategy formulation process shared with middle management?

Rarely.   □ –0

Usually only the major programs or strategies are discussed with middle-level management.   □ –1

Always.   □ –2

How much time does the typical middle manager spend in strategy formulation?

Less than one week per year.   □ –0

Between one and three weeks per year.   □ –1

More than three weeks per year.   □ –2

Do key middle managers get a chance to review and comment on proposed strategies before resources are allocated among units?

No.   □ –0

Only when they are directly affected.   □ –1

Yes, it is a formal step in our process.   □ –2

How frequently do middle-level managers delegate planning?

Usually. Upper management does little planning. □ –0

Sometimes. Delegation happens only when subordinate
staff are unusually well-informed. □ –1

Infrequently. Most managers do not delegate planning to
lower-level personnel. □ –2

*Is the planning process at the middle-management level essentially the
same as budgeting?*

Yes. Extensive use of detailed and financial forms. □ –0

Emphasis is still financial; some market consideration is
required. □ –1

No. Emphasis is on qualitative aspects, market factors,
and strategic programs. □ –2

What is the nature of the system that monitors strategic programs?

There is no system in operation. □ –0

Generally speaking, only major capital investments are
monitored on a systematic basis. □ –1

In addition to major capital investment projects, the
system monitors key markets, customers, competitors,
financial indices, and programs. □ –2

Section II

These questions concern the processes of strategy development and evaluation.

How frequent is the use of outsiders in strategy formulation?

Rare. □ –0

Occasionally used on selected technical problems. □ –1

Often use experts or consultants to lend objectivity. □ –2

*What is the nature of corporate staff support for strategy formulation
within the organization?*

None. All analyses are done at lower organizational levels. □ –0

Some. Corporate staff has minimal involvement. □ –1

A staff group exists to support and educate users in
analytic techniques for strategy formulation. □ –2

How frequently are strategic proposals critically discussed?

Rarely. Proposals are usually accepted without debate. ☐ -0

Sometimes. Proposals have been rejected, but it is rare. ☐ -1

Frequently. Proposals usually require some revision as a result of critical review. ☐ -2

How are strategic proposals reviewed internally?

There is no review process. ☐ -0

Reviews are done only on major investments or projects. ☐ -1

Most aspects of strategy are reviewed by one or more groups in the corporation. ☐ -2

How effective do managers feel the strategy formulation process is?

Ineffective. ☐ -0

Somewhat effective. ☐ -1

Very effective. ☐ -2

How much time is given to outside experts for strategy input and review?

Little or none (less than 8 hours/year). ☐ -0

Some (between 8 and 40 hours/year). ☐ -1

Substantial (over 40 hours/year). ☐ -2

What is the level of analysis supporting strategy formulation?

Conclusions are usually based on subjective reasoning. ☐ -0

Some techniques (such as growth-share matrices) are utilized, but do not rely on quantitative tools to any great degree. ☐ -1

Portfolio techniques, models as appropriate, and economic analyses are all employed. ☐ -2

How flexible is the analysis of strategies?

Uniform analysis guidelines are used for all planning units. ☐ -0

Guidelines vary somewhat by planning unit. ☐ -1

Analysis is open-ended and may be extended as circumstances dictate. ☐ -2

How are risk and uncertainty incorporated into the analysis of strategies?

A "best-guess" scenario of future economic conditions is used. ☐ –0

Several scenarios to evaluate strategies are used. ☐ –1

Risk is explicitly estimated using quantitative methods. ☐ –2

What kind of analysis of competition is done in strategy formulation and evaluation?

Little or none. ☐ –0

Some. The likely moves of a few major competitors are qualitatively estimated. ☐ –1

Both the quantitative and qualitative nature of competitors are explicitly estimated by market segment. ☐ –2

When used as a diagnostic tool, the total points associated with Section I and Section II of the questionnaire are calculated separately, reflecting their individual positions on the Exhibit 1–2 matrix. The scores for each section can be evaluated as follows:

0–4	Poor
5–8	Fair
9–12	Good
13–16	Very good
17–20	Outstanding

A company's or SBU's position can then be located on Exhibit 1–2. To illustrate, five senior-level executives in a large firm rated their company using this evaluation technique. Scores for the horizontal axis ranged from 12 to 17, with a median of 16. The vertical axis scores ranged from 6 to 10, with a median of 8. Therefore, these executives saw their firm's effectiveness with the strategy formulation process as similar to the Business-as-Usual position in Exhibit 1–2, indicating a need for improvements that will reposition the process effectively in the Winning Combination area. The major issues requiring attention are reflected by low scores on individual questions, which focus on the weaknesses in specific areas.

ANALYTICAL STEPS

While it is vital that the process of strategy formulation be well designed, the correct process by itself is not enough. Many companies are involved in more than one business. The analytical steps described here apply to each business, which are often described as strategic business units. The four major analytical steps for SBUs include:

Business definition
Economic analysis
Competitive position evaluation
Market and business unit growth analysis

It is important to understand that the analytical steps, although presented sequentially, are interactive. The analytical steps in the decision process are shown graphically in Exhibit 1-3, and each step is discussed in more detail below.

Business Definition

The first question to ask before any discussion of desired strategic change can take place is: What businesses are we in? This can raise controversy in some companies, for many different ideas of how the businesses ought to be defined may emerge, each with subtle variations that reveal different perceptions about the essence of the businesses and the factors that determine success.

Exhibit 1-3. Analytical Steps for Business Unit Strategy Formulation.

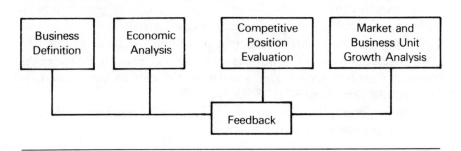

In some companies the process of discussing and reconciling conflicting ideas about business definition is discarded in favor of an initial statement prepared or approved by one or two top executives or planning staff members. But for most companies, the examination of this basic issue is useful, especially in the face of significant strategic change. Discussion of the business's definition increases the probability that more people in the organization will accept the ultimate strategy.

The business definition is the starting point in the analytical process of strategy formulation because it identifies the relevant external environments that need to be studied. The business definition includes definitions of market, function, and technology. *Market* reflects the customer groups being served; *function* refers to the customer needs being satisfied; and *technology* describes how the company's products or services satisfy customer needs.

Business Definition—By Market Served.   The important consideration in defining a business by market is the customer perspective; that is, which customer groups are being served by the company's products? Customer groups are separated by cost barriers. Consider water-treatment chemicals, for instance. The same product can have at least two significantly different uses—industrial use in water-pollution treatment, and home use in swimming pools. Exactly the same chemicals are used, but the needs of the markets being served are completely different.

Industrial treatment chemicals, furthermore, are bought in carload lots. Delivery is direct from the manufacturers, and skilled engineers apply the chemicals. For consumer pool use, on the other hand, chemicals are sold in five-, ten-, or fifty-pound bags. They are purchased from retailers and applied by homeowners. Significantly different delivery requirements, distribution channels, and information needs exist for these two customer groups. The cost of getting in position to serve either group represents a cost barrier.

Meaningful cost barriers exist in providing the same product to two different groups of customers. It is thus necessary to consider the customer groups served and what it would cost to serve any new groups the firm contemplates serving.

Another example is the computer industry. Both Burroughs and Digital Equipment Corporation have achieved success in the computer business, despite IBM's larger size. Burroughs has been successful by concentrating on certain banking applications, while Digital's focus has been on minicomputers. Each has targeted a segment of the larger market served by IBM.

Customer groups may be narrowly defined for a specialized product, particularly an industrial product. For example, airplane manufacturers are the target market for a rivet suitable only for airplanes. If other applications are possible, the proper market encompasses a larger spectrum of sheet-metal users.

For less specialized products, the definition of market is more difficult and more critical. For many years, one automobile company defined its market as the people who bought its cars; by definition, therefore, the company enjoyed a "100% share" of its market. Over time, actual units sold declined drastically, until the company redefined its market along more meaningful lines—a middle-aged consumer wanting a medium- to full-sized car with an establishment image, costing more than a Chevrolet but less than a Cadillac.

Similarly, makers of large U.S. automobiles saw their market as the U.S. auto buyer, while European and Japanese manufacturers viewed the market in worldwide terms. As everyone eventually learned, increased customer sensitivity to fuel availability and cost in the United States helped foreign automakers make rapid gains in market share, because demand grew for the cars that foreign manufacturers were already selling elsewhere around the world.

U.S. automakers are now reshaping their automobiles to conform more to to the type of car sought in worldwide markets. The need for smaller and more efficient cars had been apparent for some time to many outside observers, but the major change was eventually precipitated by foreign competition and government fuel economy regulations.

Part of the problem U.S. automakers have is financial. The long lead times and enormous investment for engineering new lines in the U.S. auto industry clashed with a shorter capital recovery cycle for model changes in larger cars. But the reluctance of U.S. automakers to shift their production emphasis was not only financial—it was reinforced by the culture and systems within the companies. The product-line structure carried great weight organizationally. In the competition for resources within the corporation, advocates of new lines of downsized cars had no entrenched organizational power. Successfully implementing a downsizing strategy required not only fundamental changes in marketing approaches and major reallocations of resources, but also changes in organization, reward systems, and culture.

Long-term success with one view of the marketplace tends to institutionalize that view within an organization. This can lead to active resistance to the adoption of new approaches, however apparent the need for change may be. In the course of defining the business by markets served, then, managers need to carefully analyze the market and decide what markets it can serve competitively. The mere understanding of the market and the company's ability to compete is not, however, adequate. It is also important to define the business by function and by technology.

Business Definition — By Function.   The need that the product fulfills is its function. The substitutability of alternative products is important in defining a business, because too narrow a definition of function ignores relevant competition. In fact, a broad definition is sometimes required to perceive the real strategic issues. A carbon paper manufacturer who defines function in a way that includes only other carbon paper manufacturers as competitors, for instance, is missing the point; photocopying machines have virtually eliminated the product in most applications. A button manufacturer, in the same way, must consider zippers, snaps, and Velcro as competitive substitutes.

A company's perception of function frequently overemphasizes the unique qualities of its own product. The consumers' definition of their needs should actually control the functional definition. By listening to consumers on a regular basis, a company can build a comprehensive and accurate composite of the user's needs that will serve well in the functional definition of the business. Consider the following case:

In the early 1960s, a company developed an instant breakfast food, and in its functional definition emphasized the independence of children in preparing their own breakfasts. Unfortunately this emphasis overlooked the common perception at that time that a good homemaker prepared breakfast for her family. Now, with that traditional role changing, this company's functional definition is more appropriate to the market.

Breadth of product capabilities also affects function in the business definition. Some products have a specialized function, and all consumers use them the same way. A tow truck has a specialized purpose, for example, whereas a van can be used in many ways, making a definition of its function more complex.

It is thus necessary to understand the total product a customer is buying. A natural tendency to focus narrowly on the physical product can lead to lack of attention to intangible attributes that consumers value highly. In many markets, powerful competitors have been eclipsed by innovators who understood that the user was interested in a product attribute—such as service or flexibility or support—previously considered unimportant. The vast growth of convenience features in retailing, packaging, and product use, for example, attest to the consumer's willingness to trade price for quality. Conversely, generic foods illustrate that many consumers will purchase a plain package and perhaps a slightly lower grade of food for a lower price.

Doing a good job of defining the business by function during the strategy formulation process will help a company focus its strategic thinking. By understanding both the market and the function of the product for the customer, the company can begin to decide how it will position itself with its products to meet the needs of the marketplace.

Business Definition—By Technology.   Technology also has a place in the definition of the business. By altering the product, technological developments can have an impact on the market and functional definitions. Changes in technology can alter economic barriers and shift the competitive balance. In the heavy aircraft engine business, for example, the technology moved from propeller to jet. The function was exactly the same. The market was exactly the same. The technology, however, was totally changed. And, because many existing firms did not properly define their business by technology, companies skilled in the new technology were generally not the same companies skilled in the old technology.

Changes in technology may alter the appropriate business definition and shift the competitive balance, as the following case example illustrates:

> Mechanical calculators filled a need for rapid, accurate calculations. When electronic calculators were introduced, fulfilling the same need using a different technology at vastly reduced cost, mechanical calculators virtually disappeared.

Strong competitors usually have large investments of capital and time in their existing technology, and they plan on long and productive lives for those assets. Their tendency is to deny the competitive threat posed by the new technology in the hope that it will not be accepted:

> A locomotive company steadfastly held to steam technology. If it had seen itself in the tractive power business and recognized the inherent advantages of diesel technology, it might be in business today. The locomotive company only stayed in business as long as it did, in fact, because of railroad management's nostalgia and reluctance to switch from coal—one of its biggest freight customers. But in the final analysis, practicality, ecomics, and reliability won out over romance, and the company went out of business.

Summary.   If a business is properly defined in terms of the customer groups served, the function served (and competitive substitutes), and the technology involved in the products, it is possible to define the firm's strategic business units. If the business is not defined properly, it is impossible to develop a coherent strategy, either at the company or SBU level.

Economic analysis is also required to determine competitive strengths for the company's businesses. By erecting barriers around the businesses, the company positions itself so that it develops unique characteristics; it therefore will be in a more powerful competitive position. The next section describes how economic analysis can be used to determine and then subsequently erect those barriers.

Economic Analysis

In the economic analysis step of strategy formulation, the marketplace is broken into relevant segments, the organization's economic strengths and weaknesses are identified, and competitive behavior is clarified. The relative attractiveness of strategic business options open to a company's SBUs can be stated as the ability of each option to produce above-average discounted cash flows in return for the resources committed to it. Such measures of attractiveness are best developed through a combination of proper business definition (as outlined above) and consideration of economic barriers surrounding the segments. The process of economic analysis must be rigorous and objective to ensure that assumptions are applied to data that accurately reflect the company's situation and capabilities.

The markets to be served are segmented into groups of products or customers based on the business definitions established earlier. An analysis of how current and potential customers use a product, often based on the functional definition, determines the needs of various customer groups, provides a basis for meeting those needs, and establishes the basis for the costs of serving each customer group. Economic barriers can be erected, but they are meaningful only if it is difficult for competitors to cross them—that is, if it is costly or impractical for them to do so.

Segmentation.   A good business definition permits an economic analysis of competitors and will help explain variations in market share and profitability within the industry. Having defined the business, it is necessary to examine market segments within that business. Rare is the opportunity to dominate all segments of a market, and companies usually have success focusing upon small segments within large markets. This focus can provide opportunities for above-average returns, even in the face of larger competitors. For example, premium scotch and scotch serve significantly different customer groups, although the product inside the bottle is essentially the same. The difference in the cost of producing premium scotch versus "no-name" scotch is much less than the price difference. A significant part of the price difference is represented by marketing.

To be a useful basis for segmentation, a group of buyers must be significant enough in purchasing volume to merit attention, substantially different from other groups in its purchase decision-making, and accessible at reasonable cost through a particular promotional medium or channel of distribution. In some situations, the cost of providing benefits to all purchasers is so low that it does not make sense to withhold them from anyone:

> Japanese car manufacturers have demonstrated with their mid-priced cars that virtually all buyers will take a clock, radio, and other extras if the price is so low as to be unimportant in the

> overall price of the car. However, where choices have to be made and marginal costs cannot be cut—with extras such as air conditioning and sunroofs—Japanese manufacturers have been increasing their model selections in response to their increased market penetration, while U.S. manufacturers have been rationalizing and consolidating their lines.

In assessing the attractiveness of a particular segment, it is important to have a working knowledge of the total cost required to serve that segment, both out-of-pocket costs and the impact on the rest of the business. This requires a close analysis of the requirements of the customers in the group. Customers may, for instance, vary by order size, need for technical support, location, or numerous other factors. Sometimes the costs of serving a segment can be prohibitvely high:

> A paint company that traditionally manufactured for inventory decided to go into custom coatings to utilize its excess production capacity. The total manufacturing and distribution margins on the custom coatings appeared to be much higher than on the inventoried lines. But disruption of production schedules caused by the unpredictable demand for custom coatings actually cost the company more in lost production than it made by using its excess production capacity.

Had the paint company looked closely at the impact of serving the custom coatings segment on its production system, it would not have considered that segment as attractive. Careful segmentation will also reveal the competitors to study, the range of products to consider, and the markets to examine.

Economic Barriers.   In a free market economy, the ability of competitors to enter and leave a business depends upon the economic barriers surrounding that business. It is therefore important to ask, "What is our advantage over our competitors?" and "How do we prevent our suppliers or buyers from becoming our competitors through forward or backward integration?"

As long as a business provides an above-average discounted cash flow, competitors will tend to enter. But why will a particular company do better than its competitors? Why don't the competitors do exactly the same thing that company is doing, thereby driving returns to a level at which the business no longer attracts capital? Finally, what would it cost competitors to overcome whatever advantages a company has? Answers to these questions can be clarified by an analysis of value-added steps involved in producing and marketing a firm's product or service.

Value Added.   Value added is the amount of additional economic benefit perceived by the customer that is provided by the company at each stage from raw material acquisition through final usage. When considering economic barriers, determining the stages where value is added to the product or service delineates the economic leverage points that will produce the greatest strategic impact. Most products can be broken down into a series of value-added steps: raw material procurement, processing, fabrication, assembly, distribution, and marketing. The proportion of value added at each stage is critical in evaluating strategic alternatives.

Strategies can be effective because the company has a monopoly on one stage of value added or because it is the low-cost producer of a stage of value added. Effective strategy can be based on absolute control over unique resources or technology, in the way that OPEC, with control over a relatively nonsubstitutable raw material, is able to overcome the oil companies' control over the refining, transportation, and distribution stages of production. Such opportunities are rare in a free market except where public policy will enforce a monopoly through patent or exclusive franchise.

More commonly, strategies can establish a company as the low-cost competitor in one *key stage* of value added. It is in that stage where the greatest advantage can be gained; disadvantages in other stages of production can be overcome or other advantages enhanced. The defensibility of this position depends upon how real the segment barriers are and on how large a portion of the product's value is added at this stage.

A superior and defensible relative cost position at a key stage of value added will be the basis for a long-term strategic advantage. A *long-term strategic advantage* provides better-than-average returns over a long period of time. *Superior* means that a company has lower costs than competitors. *Defensible* means that costs are not only lower now, but can be kept lower. *Relative cost position* refers to what it costs a company to do something compared to what it costs its competitors to do the same thing. A *key stage of value added* refers to the part of the production and delivery process where large parts of the costs are incurred.

Most products have a series of steps leading to the final product. For most products, one or another of those steps is much more important than the others in terms of costs. These important steps are the focus for maintaining a relative competitive edge.

Most products start with supplies of raw materials. In the gold-mining business, for example, the most important competitive factor to have a mine with some gold. Raw material procurement is critical. No gold: no mine, no business. On the other hand, if a rich gold mine is owned, the company is going to make money. Marketing or advertising is unimportant. Production technology is important but widely shared. The key is to produce at less than the market price. People who are successful in the gold-mining business *have good mines.*

In other businesses it is not the procurement of the raw material but their processing that provides the major portion of value added. In products such as steel or paper, there are raw materials—iron ore or pulp. Interestingly enough, Japan, which has neither iron ore nor many trees has significant steel and paper businesses. Considerable value is added not in the procurement stage, but in the processing stage. If one is relatively cost-effective in a processing stage, that effectiveness can provide an overall cost advantage.

There are businesses where fabrication—putting together the processed raw materials—is critical. It is difficult to have an advantage in the manufacture of integrated circuits, for instance, merely through efficient production of silicon. The key element is the ability to fabricate the product cheaply.

Assembly of parts can be a major stage of value added. Apparel, for example, is labor-intensive in the assembly stage. If a low-wage country has a relative cost advantage in the assembly stage, that will provide it with the relative cost advantage overall. Even though the raw cotton and cloth may be the same price, assembly of the apparel provides the bulk of the apparel cost.

Physical distribution can be critical. Consider generic bottled water. It is hard to differentiate the product. Water is bulky and thus very expensive to move, so an advantage in physical distribution provides an overall advantage in the product. Therefore, the product tends to be distributed locally.

Perrier, however, successfully branded its water and changed the business. It created a different stage of value-added marketing. In products such as branded cosmetics, liquors, and bottled water, most of the value added is not added anywhere in producing the product itself, but in selling and marketing.

The examples in Exhibit 1-4 stress the importance of relative cost position as an economic barrier and a means of segmentation for manufacturing industries. Attaining a low-cost position relative to competitors in a significant stage of value added is an effective strategy. However, defensibility of position depends not only upon how real the segment barriers are, but also on how large a portion of the value added is represented by the stage where the low-cost position is enjoyed. Changes in the technology of production or distribution, or in how the product is marketed, can induce changes in the ability of manufacturing firms to complete.

In the case of service industries, much the same reasoning applies. Economic barriers for a service-oriented firm relate to the specific skills built into the organization required to deliver the services the firm offers to consumers. Barriers arise because the firm's particular mix of skill types, quality, and extent of service cannot be duplicated easily by other companies. Although a service firm's major assets are usually its staff, even hiring away key people to a competitor will typically not allow the competitor to completely eradicate the relative cost barrier it faces in seeking to enter another firm's market.

Exhibit 1-4. Role of Relative Cost Advantages in Different Production Stages.

Value-added by production stage	Examples of products where an effective economic barrier or cost advantage is critical in this production stage
Raw material procurement	Gold mining
Raw material processing	Steel, paper
Product fabrication	Integrated circuits
Assembly	Apparel
Physical distribution	Bottled water
Marketing	Branded cosmetics, liquor

Building Strategic Barriers in Service Businesses.   Arthur Andersen, one of the Big Eight accounting firms, established economic barriers through its people development and corporate culture. Not only did Arthur Andersen restrict its services to become highly proficient in its service areas, but it followed recruiting and development policies that were designed to create a consistent approach to client service throughout this large firm. This dedicated approach and the resulting distinctive culture it produced became an extremely effective barrier to competition.

Serving different segments and meeting particular needs with given relative costs can be highlighted in a matrix like the one shown in Exhibit 1–5. Effective marketing for products with high marketing value-added can create consumer franchises that command price premiums. A combination of what it costs to do something and the kind of price premium a differentiated product commands can translate into significant differences in margins.

The matrix in Exhibit 1–5 displays relative cost on the vertical axis and degree of product differentiation on the horizontal axis. It shows low-cost versus high-cost competitors, and relatively undifferentiated commodity products versus highly differentiated branded products that can command a price premium.

The upper-right quadrant is the low-cost producer of a highly differentiated product that can command a price premium. This is an

Exhibit 1–5.   Relative Cost/Product Differentiation Matrix.

	Undifferentiated	*Highly Differentiated*
Low-cost	Chemicals	Anheuser-Busch
High-cost	Coal	Designer Jeans

excellent position. This type of business should generate substantial profits and cash flow. Anheuser-Busch, the example used, is among the lowest cost producers of beer because of regional distribution by large, efficient breweries and its ability to spread advertising costs over a national market at a lower cost per impression. Busch can also command premiums, particularly on its Michelob brand. These two factors together generate attractive profits.

The lower-left quadrant is a high-cost producer of an undifferentiated commodity product. This is a very weak position. Examples include inefficient producers of cold-rolled steel, steel plates, coal, or cement. An undifferentiated commodity cannot command any premium, and high production costs depress margins.

The other two quadrants are more interesting. The upper left is a low-cost producer of an undifferentiated commodity. Profits are possible, but a concern remains regarding the basis of the low-cost position. Is it an exhaustible resource, a particular technology, something about the process, a larger scale, or low labor costs? The only thing protecting the firm's margins is its low relative cost position, because customers have difficulty differentiating between this firm's product and that of their competitors.

Finally, consider the lower-right quadrant. The firm's products are differentiated and command price premiums, but the company is a high-cost producer. For example, a manufacturer of designer jeans clearly differentiates the product and seeks large price premiums. Even a high-cost producer can still generate considerable profits in this quadrant.

Building Economic Barriers.   An economic barrier is any costly hurdle that protects a competitive advantage a firm has in some key stage of producing, marketing, and delivering a product or service. Potential competitors are effectively denied entry by such barriers. Relevant considerations include the advantage a company may have over its competitors, why the competitors do not copy it, and what it would cost them to overcome its economic advantage. The value of economic barriers can be determined in part by considering the relative cost position of competing firms. Differences in cost positions, together with the ability to create and sustain price premiums, translate into differences in margins and, therefore, cash flows.

Relative cost position is an economic barrier greatly affected by the scale of operation, experience, and technology of the firm's facilities. More efficient technology may be employed if scale thresholds are reached. Larger scale operations are made possible by gains in market share, and increases in market share in defined markets can be a key strategic goal. Where additional share has value, this value can be calculated and compared against the cost of attaining it.

In considering the economics of a business and how economic barriers can be constructed, the relevant factors include cycles of the business that affect timing and certainty of returns on new capital investment; an historic supply-demand relationship with under- or overcapacity; the degree of fixed costs that can make extra volume inexpensive if the investment is made (or expensive if it is not); competitive scale of plants (which determines the preferred size of capacity increments); and transferability of technology to new entrants.

Close attention should be paid to the economic barrier aspects of building the company's ability to serve its customers. Because these implementation aspects are difficult to quantify and cost out, they are too frequently excluded from the analytical process, even though they can radically alter the economic assumptions on which the conclusions are based.

For example, the cost of building new or different organizational skills can be an insuperable economic barrier, particularly when the company's culture works against the change. A company with a production orientation and a tradition of cost control must think twice before planning to enter a market segment where service, responsiveness to customer needs, and technical support are required in the marketing effort. Such skills are very difficult and slow to build, and they could not be delivered successfully without a different management and control structure. A strong competitive firm will build the relevant organizational skills to create effective barriers around itself.

In formulating strategy, it is vital to set strategic objectives, to define the businesses the company wishes to be in, and to determine ways to erect barriers to entry. This is the beginning of the process of building a competitive advantage. But what about the competition? The next section describes analytical tools for evaluating the company's competitive position.

Evaluating Competitive Position

Performance relative to competitors is the essential test of business success. In strategy formulation, the strengths and behaviors of competitors are examined to determine the competitive position they hold in the marketplace and which ways they are likely to move given various trends and events. The actions of competitors will have a direct effect on the success of any strategy.

An analysis of the competitive situation includes a determination of how competitors segment the market and approach the customer. Sometimes this reveals opportunities. Examining the economics of a product may indicate that concentration on a narrow, high-volume line can offer substantial economies that will permit aggressive pricing of items. A competitor providing a broad product line may spread a large proportion of common costs across the line. In other circumstances, competitors may offer a range of support services such as education, training, maintenance, and application engineering. The cost of such services is built into the price of the product. Large-volume users may not require them, and they represent an opportunity to offer a stripped-down version at a reduced price.

Relative competitive position is an indicator of relative costs. Greater market share provides an opportunity to spread marketing costs, develop production scale economies, and accumulate know-how in production and distribution.

In analyzing the competition, the market is defined to include product substitutes and customer needs. This market segment describes the area around which economic barriers can be built. Within a particular market segment, it is useful to understand which competitors are gaining share, because this reveals patterns of investment, allocation of resources, and perceptions of the attractiveness of the business. Changes in share can also predict relative cost positions in the future.

Past behavior is frequently an indication of how competitors will react to a company's future actions. Past reactions to changes in price schedules, additions to capacity, changes in technology, or expansion of marketing territory or market share reveal potential future responses.

Taking into consideration the implementation aspects of a competitor's strategy can be valuable in evaluating its current and future position. For example, a conservative, traditionally risk-averse competitor will almost certainly have trouble implementing a strategy that prescribes broad diversification outside of its industry.

One way to gain an understanding of potential implementation difficulties and opportunities of a competitor is to do some extensive role-playing with knowledgeable associates. Each assumes the role of a counterpart in the competition and discusses the strategy as if he or she worked for the competition. This kind of activity will often reveal implementation weaknesses of the competition that the company may be able to exploit.

If a competitor is in only one business, it probably has to fund its growth from internally generated cash. If it starts to lose share to other competitors, even though its absolute sales may be growing, relative profitability and cash flow are probably already below the competition and may get worse.

When a competitor is an operating unit of a larger company, understanding something about the parent company's business portfolio strategy and its perception of the particular operating unit is necessary. If the parent lets units reinvest according to their cash flows, the competitive operating unit should be viewed as an independent, small company. If the parent reallocates cash among divisions to maximize return from the entire portfolio, then it depends on the competing unit's rate of return compared to other units, and on the parent's cost of capital. If a business is seen by the parent as particularly promising, the unit may be allowed to spend cash beyond amounts typically generated in the industry so that it can invest further in advanced technology, market development, and working capital growth to become a formidable competitor in the future.

Strategies for low-growth and high-growth markets are different but, in both cases, market share is recognized as having a high positive correlation with profitability. Higher market share offers economies of scale in production, distribution, and marketing, as well as providing learning curve advantages. Attempts at gaining market share in mature and low-growth markets are often difficult. Gains must be at the expense of entrenched competitors who are likely to react vigorously to declines in their sales. Without some obvious competitive advantage on one side, battles for share are often long, drawn-out struggles of little net value, even to the winner.

Market and Business Unit Growth Analysis

Relative competitive position in the market being served is an important indicator of costs. Greater share provides an opportunity to spread marketing costs, develop production scale economies, and accumulate know-how in production and distribution. A useful tool to evaluate growth relative to the market is a market-growth/business-unit-growth graph (see Exhibit 1-6), sometimes called the growth/ growth model. This indicates how fast a business unit's sales are growing compared to the overall rate of growth for the market in which the unit competes. Exhibit 1-6 can be used to examine the competitive dynamics of a market situation. It can also be used to determine how one business unit behaves with respect to its portfolio of businesses.

Appendix A shows in more detail how the market-growth/business-unit-growth chart can help identify the strategies of individual business units within a given competitor. Four generic strategies of competitors are described, as noted on the following page:

Exhibit 1-6.   Market-Growth/Business-Unit-Growth Chart.

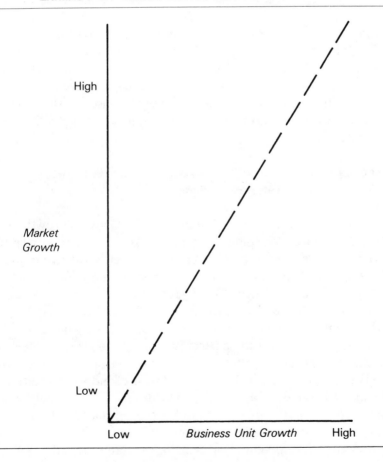

Uniform growth goals no matter how fast the market is growing. This implies that the competitor will invest enough in each business unit to achieve uniform growth. It indicates that certain high-growth markets will be neglected by the competitor, and shows another company where it can profitably invest.

Investment based on cash-generating capabilities of the individual business unit. In this case the competitor is likely to invest most heavily in its low-growth, high-cash-generating business units. This implies an opportunity to compete effectively with those units in high-growth markets.

Laissez-faire policy regarding investment. This situation is often found in firms run as holding companies, where business units are left to decide for themselves how much to invest. In this case, historical patterns of investment may provide clues about competitive behavior.

Conscious allocation of resources based on growth opportunities. Here, competitors invest in business units with above-average growth potential, and disinvest in low-growth businesses. This kind of rational competitor is the most difficult to compete with, because its allocation of resources is heavily biased toward the most attractive opportunities—opportunities that are attractive to all competitors.

Appendix A describes the approach to market-growth/business-unit-growth analysis in greater detail.

Implications of the Growth/Growth Model.   Growth/growth analysis is very helpful for understanding market movements over time and how competitors interact with one another. Effective organizations adapt to demands that different market and company growth conditions place upon them. During rapid growth, for instance, managers are encouraged to take the initiative to meet opportunities. An entrepreneurial management style is encouraged, because centralized decision-making during these periods is usually too slow to meet rapidly changing conditions. Often a combination of new competitors, unsettled channels of distribution, and lack of industry tradition results in a variety of marketing approaches in different parts of the same business. This demands flexible decision-making. Many small investments must be made at the operating level with a keen understanding of future potential or evolving customer needs.

Under conditions of market maturity and lower growth expectations, on the other hand, organizational demands are different. If the orientation has been toward high growth, some difficult adjustments have to be made. Reward systems are needed that redirect behavior toward producing profits and cash flow rather than increasing volume. Management must become more structured and control-oriented as the success factors shift from innovation toward efficiency. This requires more elaborate management processes that both organize data-gathering and decision-making and also enforce company policies and procedures.

Even the behavior and career goals of managers must be changed to remain compatible with demands of managing a low-growth business for maximum returns. If change is sudden and not well-anticipated, serious management and morale problems can develop as creative, entrepreneurial managers attempt to use particular skills and styles they have developed that no longer have any value to the firm's strategy. They may ostracize newcomers brought in to help implement a change in direction, and are certain to feel doubly betrayed by a sense of pride and ownership in the business they helped build, which they see as being handed over to people with no sense of history and without their accumulated skills.

STRATEGY FORMULATION—IN PERSPECTIVE

Corporate management's task is not only to ensure that good business strategies are developed, but also to decide how all the business unit strategies fit together in a corporate strategy. The development of corporate strategies should be undertaken once a year when all business unit data are available. Chapers 5 and 6 on planning and programming describe that process.

This chapter has concentrated on both the process by which strategy is formulated and the analytical steps required to formulate business unit strategy. But the process by which strategy is formulated must be appropriately organized. The strategy and its implementation will be very difficult unless the process is designed to include line and staff managers who have both a strategic and implementation orientation, and adopt a data-based analytical approach.

The analytical steps must include vigorous attention to objective-setting, business definition, economic analysis, competitive position evaluation, and resource allocation. These steps, together with an effective process that takes into account implementation factors covered in the remaining chapters of this book, will provide the basis for a sound strategy.

SELECTED REFERENCES

Abell, D.F. *Defining the Business: The Starting Point of Strategic Planning.* Englewood Cliffs, N.J.: Prentice-Hall, 1980.

———— , and J.S. Hammond. *Strategic Market Planning: Problems and Analytical Approaches.* Englewood Cliffs, N.J.: Prentice-Hall, 1979.

Andrews, K.R. *Concept of Corporate Strategy.* Rev. ed. Homewood, Ill.: Dow Jones-Irwin, 1980.

Ansoff, H. Igor. *Corporate Strategy.* New York: McGraw-Hill, 1965.

Boston Consulting Group. *Perspectives on Experience.* Boston: BCG, 1972.

Day, George S. "Strategic Market Analysis: Top-Down or Bottom-Up?" Working Paper. Cambridge, Mass.: Marketing Science Institute, 1980.

———— . "Diagnosing the Product Portfolio." *Journal of Marketing* (April 1977).

Hamermesh, Richard G., and Stephen B. Silk. "How to Compete in Stagnant Industries." *Harvard Business Review* (September/October, 1979).

Kotler, Philip. *Marketing Management.* 4th ed. Englewood Cliffs, N.J.: Prentice-Hall, 1980.

Porter, Michael. *Competitive Strategy: Techniques for Analyzing Industries and Competitors.* New York: Free Press, 1980.

Vancil, Richard F. *Decentralization: Managerial Ambiguity by Design.* Homewood, Ill.: Dow Jones-Irwin, 1978.

———— . "Strategy Formulation in Complex Organizations." *Sloan Management Review* (Winter 1976).

2 CULTURE

*OK, you've convinced me that we need to change
our strategic direction. But how will I ever convince my people to value innovation and entrepreneurship when, for twenty-five years, tradition,
loyalty, and past success stories have dominated
our product development effort?*—President, large
chemical manufacturer.

In the overall context of implementing strategy (see Exhibit 2–1), the
element of culture—although very important—is no doubt the most
nebulous and difficult to grasp. It is clear, however, that most organizations develop unique cultures, and that a specific culture has a
direct impact on how well—and in many cases, whether or not—a
particular strategy can be implemented. Recognizing the existence of
culture and understanding its implications are necessary steps when
contemplating the implementation of strategic change. While it is important to realize when a particular strategy might be constrained by
a firm's culture, it is equally important to recognize the positive
strengths of the culture—those forces that have brought success to
the organization—and build on them for the future.

While reading this chapter, it will be useful to keep in mind the following questions:

What is corporate culture?

How well does the current culture match existing strategies?

When contemplating a change in strategy, what aspects of culture
   need to be considered?

Exhibit 2-1.   Implementing Strategy: Culture.

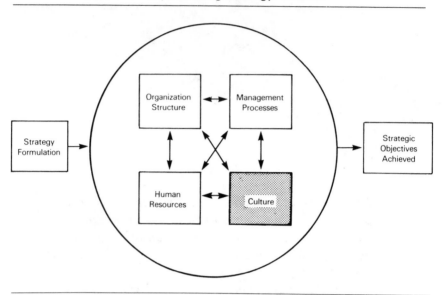

If asked to name a few of the best-run companies, one would in-clude the star performers so often referred to in articles about good management and organization—GE, IBM, Texas Instruments, as well as Mitsubishi, Sony, ICI, Phillips, and Siemens. Any discussion of what makes these firms stars will include their strategic sense, clear organization, management systems, and excellent people at the top. In addition, the well-run corporations of the world are known to have distinctive cultures that are an integral part of their ability to create, implement, and maintain corporate positions of world lead-ership.

Coca-Cola and Pepsi, Hertz and Avis, Mars and Hershey are direct competitors within their industries. No doubt their strategies differ significantly. And so do their companies' cultures. All one has to do to get a feel for the different cultures of competing businesses is to spend a day in each, observing patterns of variations in dress, jargon, and style. But there is something else—there are characteristic ways of making decisions, relating to bosses, and choosing people to fill key jobs.

These routines buried deep in a company's culture are the most ac-curate reflections of why things work the way they do, and why one firm succeeds with its strategies where another fails. Evaluating an organization's culture can thus be critical when managing an organization through a period of strategic change.

Numerous examples exist where a corporate culture that was once a source of strength has become a major obstacle to future success:

> As widely reported in the business press, AT&T announced in 1978 that it was making a major strategic shift from a service-oriented telephone utility to a market-oriented communications business. Its chairman went on intracompany TV to announce to every employee, "We will become a marketing company." To implement this new strategy, AT&T has undertaken the largest organizational transformation in the history of U.S. industry. Of the one million jobs at AT&T, one out of every three will be changed.
>
> Despite the major changes in structure, in human resources, and in support systems, there is a general consensus, both inside and outside AT&T, that its greatest task in making its strategy succeed will be to transform the corporation's culture. For many years the culture of the corporation has developed in the context of a regulated monopoly, which directly influenced the manner in which decisions were made, structures were set, people were chosen, and management processes run. To change this culture so that it fits effectively in its new competitive environment is a formidable task that will take years to accomplish.

This raises the question, How can a company get a handle on its culture? Some have been frustrated in their attempts:

> For six years, the president of a large corporation attempted to turn around a firm that suffered from an overabundance of unprofitable products that could not, it seemed, be cut; from antiquated plant and equipment that could not be written off; and from the entrenched manufacturing bias of the board sitting in the capital-goods-oriented city of Cleveland. Speaking of his attempts to transform the company from a production-oriented firm to a marketing-oriented one, the president said, "When you take a 100-year-old company and change the culture of the organization and try to do that in Cleveland's traditional busi-

> ness setting—well, it takes time. You just have to keep hammer-
> ing away at everybody." After six years of such "hammering
> away," the president resigned saying the job was no longer any
> fun. He had dented, but not substantially reshaped, the culture.

Corporate cultures have a powerful influence on managers' behavior. As the above examples suggest, when a business is shifting its
strategic direction, its culture may be a source of strength or weakness. Yet it is possible to evaluate this elusive aspect of organization
that appears to be linked so intimately with strategic success or failure.
The likely impact an organization's culture will have on the chances
for success of future business strategies can be gauged, as the following sections illustrate.

DEFINING CULTURE

Within companies there are characteristic ways of conducting interpersonal relationships. Decision-making, problem-solving, and selecting people to fill jobs are parts of corporate behavior that differ
markedly from one company to another. Within a large company, in
fact, there may be cultural differences between departments or divisions.

Culture is much more than management style. It can be identified
as the way an organization performs a given set of tasks. It is the set
of traditional and habitual ways of thinking, feeling, and reacting to
opportunities and problems that confront an organization. It is rooted
in the past successes and failures of the organization—and successes
provide models to follow in the future, while failures provide models
to avoid. Culture is also an emotional bond that holds an organization together. But an emotion does not lend itself to evaluation by
quantitative and analytical techniques like those that can be used to
assess strategy formulation, organizational structures, human resources, or management processes.

One way to grasp what culture is might be to understand what it is
not. Many large corporations periodically undertake climate surveys
that "take the temperatures" of their organizations. But climate is
not culture. Climate is a measure of whether people's expectations of
their work environment in an organization are being met. Measure-

ments of climate can be very helpful in pinpointing the causes of poor employee motivation, such as unclear organizational goals, dissatisfaction with compensation, inadequate advancement opportunities, or biased promotion practices. Actions to address these sources of dissatisfaction tend to improve motivation. Improved motivation ought to result in improved performance and, by and large, the evidence suggests that it does.

Culture, on the other hand, is a pattern of beliefs and expectations shared by the members of an organization. These beliefs and expectations produce rules for behavior—norms—that powerfully shape the behavior of individuals and groups in the organization. So while climate measures whether expectations are being met, culture is concerned with the nature of those expectations.

CULTURAL FIT

Different companies have different cultures. The culture of an organization is assimilated by its employees, and those who cannot accept the culture often choose or are asked to leave. Some organizations, for instance, develop an informal atmosphere that values worker creativity; others evolve formal, structured environments that maintain and value higher productivity.

A strategy may be brilliantly formulated, suited to the competitive situation, and supported by adequate financial and human resources. Management processes may be highly integrated and well-established throughout the company. But how well the strategy fits with the remaining element, culture, will undoubtedly affect the success of the strategy.

In some cases, then, a corporate strategy matches its culture and helps the firm achieve its strategy:

> IBM is a company totally dedicated to a marketing concept that focuses on service. That focus distinguishes IBM from most of its competitors and has favorably impressed the consumer.

In other cases, corporate culture is a barrier to the successful implementation of a strategy:

AT&T also has a strong service orientation. In the early 1960s, an attempt to develop a marketing orientation failed because the training effort did not consider that the firm's culture was based on a set of values very different from what was being taught. Training emphasized customized sales, while the culture was oriented to noncustomized, mass sales. Past corporate success with the old techniques eliminated any incentive to change.

Thus corporate culture can either be a help or a hinderance to implementing strategy. Although the fit is intangible, it is nonetheless critical for success.

ASSESSING CULTURAL RISK

When a business contemplates a change in strategic direction, its culture will be a source of strength or weakness, and sometimes both. The degree to which corporate culture has an impact on corporate strategy is the strategy's *cultural risk.*

Strategic needs develop into action plans that an organization follows to challenge the competition. Each individual within the organization maintains beliefs about the appropriateness, feasibility, and chance for success of the action plans. Cultural risk results when there is a conflict between the action plans and these beliefs.

Exhibit 2-2 is a simple two-by-two matrix that can illustrate the cultural risks involved when an organization is contemplating a particular strategy. Potential strategic payoff of that strategy is ranked as high or low on the vertical axis, and the compatibility of the strategy with the established culture—or its cultural fit—is ranked as good or poor on the horizontal axis.

It becomes immediately apparent that the cultural risk of a strategy will be highest where its fit with the culture is poor—on the right side of the matrix. On the left side, when the strategic payoff is high and the strategy's fit with culture is good, the strategy can be positioned in box 1. Having a high-payoff strategy that meshes with the present culture is clearly the best position to be in.

A strategy of relatively low potential payoff and good cultural fit can be placed in box 2. This strategy's chances for success in the culture are good, albeit with somewhat minor overall consequences.

Exhibit 2-2. Culture/Strategy Risk Matrix.

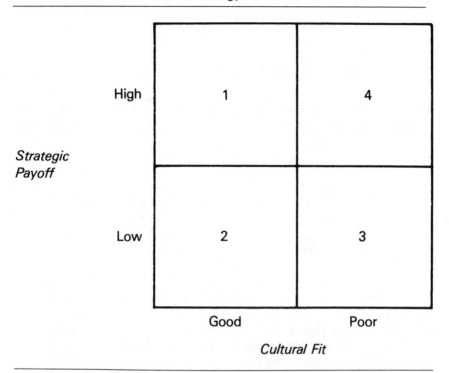

For example, a change in the management reporting system to include additional profit/loss information presents low risk when the organization already values that information. The low risk, however, is offset by the fact that the action is of minor strategic importance.

Strategies falling in box 3 are those with a low strategic payoff and poor cultural fit. Attempting to implement such strategies almost guarantees failure. Suppose, for instance, that a successful firm has never emphasized individual budget responsibility. Changing this emphasis may have some benefits, but in this organization, managerial resistance and even subversion of this attempt at marginal improvement is likely. Such strategies are best abandoned.

A strategy that falls into box 4 presents the most difficulty for managers. As its placement on the matrix illustrates, this strategy is highly desirable (or even necessary), but its fit with the present culture is poor. A manager faced with this situation basically has three choices: ignore the culture and plunge ahead; manage around it by reformulating the strategy and designing an organization that seeks to minimize cultural conflict; or changing the culture to fit the strategy.

IGNORING THE CULTURE

Ignoring the culture nearly always invites failure. When two organizations with different cultures merge, for example, results may fall short of expectations:

> The Rockwell-North American merger in 1968 was sought by both firms for its synergistic potential. Rockwell saw North American as a source of useful ideas. North American was attracted by Rockwell's commercial manufacturing and marketing.
>
> Four years after the merger, some markets failed to develop as expected and there were problems in bridging the two cultures. The aerospace people weren't accustomed to commercial problems, and worked to develop products that were overdesigned or for which there was no market. The North American president felt that it was essential to continue its basic lines of business—aerospace engineering. Rockwell's culture looked at the world as a place where profit margins dominate decision-making; North American's Ph.D.'s spent only 20% of their time on company business and were free to devote the rest as they chose on basic research.
>
> In the decade since the merger, Rockwell continued to have problems with its strategy of capitalizing on North American's scientific strengths to develop important new commercial business. Poor cultural fit restricted the ability of the firms to implement the desired strategy.

When attempting to implement a change in strategy, ignoring the culture almost inevitably leads to failure, no matter how good the strategy looks in the planning stage. As with all other elements of an organization, there must be a good fit between the culture and the chosen strategy.

MANAGING AROUND CULTURE

Managing around the culture of an organization is perhaps the most commonly observed behavior when dealing with the strategy/culture fit. Managing around culture involves identifying areas of poor fit and making accommodations to them that will not seriously affect the strategy and will increase the likelihood of a strategy's success. To lessen the gap between current culture and desired new behavior, for instance, an enhanced planning function may substitute for developing a centralized decision-making authority. Alternatively, and more directly, training managers and hiring new personnel can bring new ideas into the firm:

A small professional service firm recruited a senior staff member from its competition to help change the firm's culture from valuing qualitative analysis to also valuing rigorous quantitative analysis for its clients. The effect was disruptive to the culture initially but, over a two-year period, there has been a marked transfer of the quantitative approach to the rest of the staff.

To further illustrate the action implications of managing around a firm's culture, Exhibit 2–3 outlines typical strategies that three companies might pursue (Col. 1), and a typical approach to implementing each strategy (Col. 2). Column 3 of the exhibit summarizes a number of the cultural aspects that would form barriers to implementation. In each case, none of the typical approaches is compatible with the company's culture. The fourth column presents alternative approaches that could accomplish the same ends for each firm but are more compatible with their cultures.

Managers in a company are best able to determine the most appropriate options for managing around culture. Generally speaking, an appropriate degree of specialization, coordination, and motivation is needed. A limited number of options are available to achieve each objective, but there is flexibility. Thinking of a company in terms of the five elements presented in this book—strategy formulation, organization structure, management processes, human resources, and culture—helps.

Exhibit 2-3. Managing Around Culture.

	(1) Contemplated Strategy	(2) Typical Approaches	(3) Existing Cultural Barriers	(4) Alternative Approaches
Company A	Product/market diversification	Divisional organization	Centralized power Functional staff Hierarchical structure	Business teams
Company B	Extend a technology to new markets	Matrix organization	Multiple power centers Functional focus of staff	Progam coordinators Planning committees Greater top-management involvement
Company C	Withdraw gradually from declining market Maximize cash throw-offs	Modify reward system High visibility to top management	New-business driven Reward for innovation	Sell out

CHANGING A FIRM'S CULTURE

Changing culture is complex, expensive, and does not happen overnight. Yet some firms must change if they are to be able to respond adequately to competitive or internal pressures. Even after several years, the old culture will not disappear entirely, but it can be changed successfully:

AT&T's move to change its culture from a service-oriented utility to a market-oriented communications business is requiring significant changes in organization structure, human resources, reporting systems, and strategy, as well as a fundamental change in the way people think about their employer. Employees are being encouraged to act as entrepreneurs rather than as individuals protected by a regulated industry.

There are three prerequisites for changing culture:

1. The strategy and all its elements must be explicitly stated and easily understandable.
2. The current culture must be analyzed and made tangible.
3. Strategy must be reviewed in the context of the culture to determine where the cultural risks are.

An organization's culture is best altered by gradually reducing perceived differences between current norms and the new behavior, increasing the value placed on adaptability, and enhancing managers' ability to effect the desired change. Strong top leadership creates the pressure for change; new top management behavior sets the example.

Managers cannot be expected to change the manner in which they approach their tasks and relationships until they know the behavior required in the new culture, and what will enhance their personal development in the firm. In short, they must know how to behave and be rewarded for behaving appropriately. Changing culture requires coordination with other planned internal changes in management processes and organizational structure. The company's reward system is a valuable tool in effective cultural change, particularly when utilized in conjunction with an intensive management education program with pilot programs for implementing new strategy under controlled conditions (see Chapter 8).

In these activities, it is important to set priorities that focus on strategically significant issues while concentrating on elements of the culture where change is critical to success. In fact, it may not be desirable to totally change the culture—only those parts of it that demonstrate high cultural risk.

How Changes in Culture Are Accomplished

Change in culture begins with a review of the key cultural issues facing the company. Although an elaborate psychological profile is not necessary, the perspectives of the people who are part of the culture represent a critical factor.

Key cultural issues include the degree to which managers buy into the existing or new strategy. Buying-in implies more than tacit support. It means that managers feel that the strategy belongs to them and not to the planning group or outside consultants.

In the human resources area, the "rules of the game" that enable the organization to achieve its goals are examined. A rapidly growing organization that is recruiting extensively may have difficulty maintaining an informal communication system as it grows larger, for example, and the communication system is essential to support the creative talents of its staff.

Finally, culture influences the degree to which an organization can respond to signals provided by management systems. For example, a performance/zero-defect engineering culture may not operate very effectively under a stringent cost-measurement and control system.

CORPORATE CULTURE: IN PERSPECTIVE

When implementing a new strategy, ignoring culture is an approach that invites disaster. Managing around it may be the most realistic course for an organization in the short term. Over the long term, a change in culture may be necessary, but it is critical to plan for extensive training and management development as well as a continuous retooling of existing management processes, recruiting and even perhaps firing some individuals and reevaluating the organization's structure.

So far, corporate culture has been discussed in a post-strategy-formulation context. However, it is the perceptive chief executive who elects to address the issue of culture before it becomes a barrier to implementing strategy. There are several areas in which cultural analysis at the front end can pay dividends later.

During strategy formulation, as outlined in Chapter 1, strategies are built on management's assumption about many external factors. But a corporation's culture may cloud top managers' perspectives, often limiting the strategic options they are prepared to consider seriously. Defining the central value of a company's culture can remove old taboos that have unnecessarily constrained past strategic decision-making.

As culture conditions the direction of a company's strategic choices, a competitor's own culture conditions its strategic decisions and the effectiveness of implementation. Understanding a competitor's corporate culture can provide useful clues to how that firm will behave in the competitive environment.

Front-end consideration of culture can also be useful for rapidly growing companies. For example, high-technology firms sometimes find that the ideals and values of the founding group or individual are lost as the culture becomes institutionalized through formalized structures, reporting systems, and controls. Managing the process of cultural formation in relationship to the more tangible aspects of organization can help preserve the original driving force of the company.

The failure to successfully integrate the disparate cultures of merging companies, as in the previously cited North American-Rockwell example, often causes problems in turnover and productivity. Early definition of culture in both companies, and identification of cultural compatibility and cultural risk, would have facilitated a smoother transitional period and realization of the desired synergy.

Every corporation has a culture (which often includes several subcultures) that exerts powerful influences on the behavior of managers. For better or worse, corporate culture has a major impact on a company's ability to carry out objectives and plans, especially when a company is shifting its strategic direction.

Awareness and agreement within the company about the culture phenomenon and its effect is a vital point of departure for dealing with it. Although getting one's hands on a company's culture is a little like putting one's hands into a cloud, there is a three-step methodology for capturing the effects of culture and enabling management to deal with it more effectively.

Step 1: Define the relevant culture and subcultures in the organization. Use individual and small-group meetings. Develop a list of simply stated beliefs about "the way it is" in the organization and of current standards for how to behave. Feed these back until there is consensus around the central norms in the culture.

Step 2: Assess the risk the company's culture presents to the realization of the planned strategic effort. This is done by specifying how important and how compatible the intended organizational approaches are with the intended strategy. Using Exhibit 2-2 enables the evaluator to differentiate the risks current corporate culture presents to a proposed strategy.

Step 3: Identify and focus on those specific aspects of the company's culture that are both highly important to strategic success and incompatible with the organizational approaches that are planned. It will then be possible to develop alternative organizational approaches that better fit the existing culture, and to design planned programs to change those aspects of culture that are the source of the problem.

Matching Strategy and Culture

To match corporate culture and business strategy, the procedures above should become a part of a corporation's strategic implementation process. These steps can be taken in as sophisticated or informal a manner as desired. External consultants or internal staff support may be used, or the relevant executive from CEO on down may undertake them. Baseline descriptions of the important aspects of culture, especially in major business units expected to make significant shifts in strategy, can be prepared by line managers with the help of strategic planning and human resources staffs. An advantage of this approach is that it provides a more effective way to integrate human resources perspectives into the strategy implementation process.

SELECTED REFERENCES

"Corporate Culture: The Hard-to-Change Values That Spell Success or Failure." *Business Week,* October 27, 1980.

McGregor, Douglas. *The Human Side of Enterprise.* New York: McGraw-Hill, 1960.

Ouchi, William G. *Theory Z.* Reading, Mass.: Addison-Wesley, 1981.

Pettigrew, Andrew M. "On Studying Organizational Cultures." *Administrative Science Quarterly* (December 1979).

Schwartz, Howard M., and Stanley M. Davis. "Matching Corporate Culture and Business Strategy." *Organizational Dynamics* (Winter 1981).

Vancil, Richard F. *Decentralization: Managerial Ambiguity by Design.* Homewood, Ill.: Dow Jones-Irwin, 1978.

Watson, Thomas J. *A Business and Its Beliefs.* New York: McGraw-Hill, 1963.

Wright, J. Patrick. *On a Clear Day You Can See General Motors.* New York: Avon, 1980.

3 ORGANIZATION STRUCTURE

The company has reorganized again—it's an annual event, almost like planning and budgeting. It's funny, though. Senior management keeps moving the boxes on the organization chart around, and still things stay the same.—Planning officer in a money center bank.

When referring to organization, most managers will talk about the structure of their company—the unique arrangement of reporting relationships and responsibilities found within a particular firm. When asked to describe their organizations, they typically talk from organization charts. An organization's structure is, however, more than boxes and arrows on a chart. As shown in the model presented once again in Exhibit 3-1, an organization's structure must match, or "fit," the firm's strategy. It must also be in tune with the human resources, culture, and management processes required to move the firm toward its stated objectives. When properly done, changes in organization can be a powerful tool with which to implement a new strategy.

While we are apparently moving in this book *from* strategy formulation *to* the question of the organization's structure, the reality is—as with all the elements described in this book—that questions of the organization's structure are asked and answered on an on-going basis, in response to both internal and external environmental forces. Strategy is not formulated in a vacuum. It should consider both today's organization structure and any future changes required to implement the chosen strategy. To clarify the place of an organization's

Exhibit 3-1.   Implementing Strategy: Organization Structure.

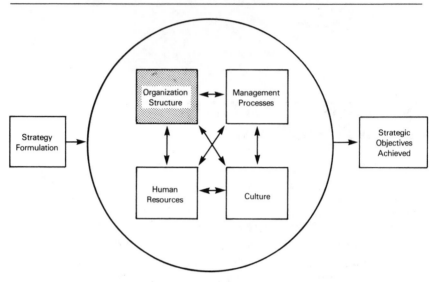

structure in our model, then, we can state that an organization's success depends both on its ability to define strategy and respond to important forces operating in its external environment, *and* on having the appropriate structures required to manage the complex internal activities that will move the firm toward its strategic goals. To see this clearly, major questions to consider in reading this chapter include:

How does the structure of the organization fit with its strategy?

In what ways do people fit the organization's structure?

Which aspects of the structure frustrate or foster desired behavior, such as communication?

How can structure be used as a strategic weapon?

CHOICE OF STRUCTURES

"It all depends." That is the response of many organization theorists and practitioners when they consider alternative structures. They say that an organization must respond to the particular demands of its external environment, as well as to a unique set of internal factors, including its strategic objectives, and that the question of structure can best be answered by reviewing structural types and their applications in particular settings.

Traditional views of organization are relatively static. Structure is very often designed after a strategy is chosen, and remains in place until another strategy is formulated. Frequently, however, by the time the new organization is fine-tuned, another strategy has already been undertaken that renders the current structure obsolete.

An alternative view, and the one taken in this book, is that organization is much more dynamic. As noted earlier, developing a strategy and an organization structure to match should be simultaneous events, not independent and sequential. When strategy is developed, therefore, organizational issues must be included as an integral part of the strategy formulation and implementation processes.

TRADITIONAL STRUCTURES

There are two major issues that need to be asked when designing or changing an organization's structure. The first one deals with the dynamic interaction of strategy and structure—How can structure be set up to carry out a strategy? The second issue involves the tradeoff between the economies of scale of a centralized organization and the responsiveness and flexibility of a decentralized structure. Each of the four structures presented in this chapter involves such tradeoffs.

Companies are commonly organized on the basis of one of four major structures:

Centralized functional
Division
Holding company
Matrix

The description of each structure features two concepts—specialization and coordination—that reflect different ways to organize around important tasks.

Centralized Functional Structure

The centralized functional organization is made up of specialized units—marketing, sales, production, engineering, R&D, personnel, finance, and administration—each with a single manager at the top (see Exhibit 3–2). Power is centralized, with a single chain of command reporting to each functional head, who in turn reports to the general manager (CEO). In an organization run by specialists who have worked their way to the top by being the "best marketer" or "best accountant" or "best production head," there is a tendency to resist delegating authority. Decisions tend to flow upward from the level where the information needed to make the decision exists. The specialization that develops in this structure is most effective when the company sells a single product or a very few products.

Maintaining communication is important in a centralized functional organization because tasks are split among a number of groups whose efforts must be directed. Because all of the activities are specialized, functions have a tendency to become internally oriented, and the necessary external coordination of tasks may not occur. Benefits that result from specialization can be negated if resources are not in the right place at the right time. If manufacturing and sales are out of balance, for example, the company suffers a loss in revenue from missed sales or the unnecessary increase in cost of excess inventory.

In a centralized functional organization, therefore, committees, teams, or other integrating devices must be used to exchange information and coordinate activities if decisions are to be made lower in the organization. But such actions require a conscious decision and the cohesive support of top management.

Exhibit 3-2.   Centralized Functional Structure.

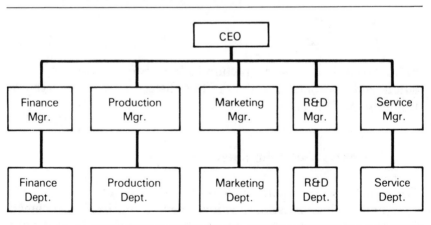

A company with a single product offering can use a centralized functional structure to its advantage. For example:

> When a major company purchased a brewery as part of its diversification effort, the impact was felt throughout the industry. Regional brewers, with fewer resources than were available to the newly acquired company, were at a disadvantage because the acquired firm now had significant economies of scale and access to centralized marketing expertise. As a result, many of the regionals went out of business.
>
> One regional brewer, however, expanded its distribution and enhanced its marketing activities while maintaining its centralized functional structure. The strategy did not require a reorganization, but it did require a refocus within the company. The reallocation effort was successful, and the regional brewer remains a strong competitor in certain markets.

Because specialization is focused on functional areas rather than on markets, products, or geography, a centralized functional organization is often constrained in the number and variety of tasks it can do simultaneously:

> A major New York brokerage house was a functionally structured business that subsequently restructured to gain focus on its two very different businesses. The firm was originally organized by function: marketing, operations, administration, capital markets. Yet the organization served two major markets—retail and institutional. Because the markets were different and priorities were unclear, confusion resulted. To resolve the ambiguity, the company reorganized to a market-based divisional structure, which removed much of the conflict and allowed management to measure the results achieved by each business.

In summary, a centralized functional structure is most appropriate in a company that produces and sells one or a few related products. Even some very large companies like IBM use this structure because they have a narrow product focus and wish to emphasize economies of scale.

To be effective, centralized functional structures are augmented by committees, task forces, and other techniques designed to foster communications to coordinate the efforts of the individual functional areas. The structure is not generally appropriate in companies that serve multiple unrelated markets. In those kinds of companies a division structure is usually more effective. Thus, as firms diversify away from a single product line or few markets, their new strategic objectives typically require a different organization structure.

Division Structure

A division structure emphasizes a decentralized organization based on product or market groupings, each managed by a general manager who reports to a division or group head (see Exhibit 3-3). The structure often mirrors the definitions of the business. Each division has its own dedicated functional resources. In some companies, where economies of scale or scarce resources dictate, divisions share marketing personnel or production capacity. Divisions compete with one another for investment capital and other corporate resources. There is also generally a headquarters staff that provides some services to the divisions and carries out corporate tasks. In some large companies, groups or sectors are developed to help rationalize the overall activities of the divisions and provide a coordinating vehicle.

Companies in the oil industry have long been dominant-product businesses with a division structure, and Exxon is representative:

Exxon's principal business includes exploring for and producing crude oil and natural gas, manufacturing petroleum and chemicals, and transporting and selling crude oil, natural gas, and petroleum and chemical products.

As far back as the 1960s, the company began to recognize that oil and gas reserves would be inadequate to meet the world's need for energy. With this in mind, Exxon undertook the strategic shift that was accelerated by OPEC activity of the mid-1970s—a shift from being a petroleum company to becoming an energy company. It created a multidivisional structure organized around related products rather than a dominant product. Consequently, its divisions now include coal mining, coal research and synthetics, nuclear energy, oil shale, solar and fuel cells, and others.

Exhibit 3-3.   Division Structure.

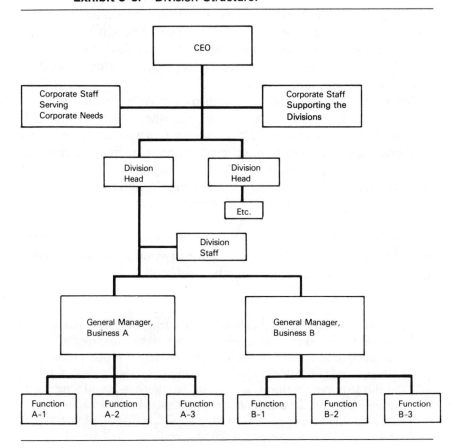

Communication in the division structure is more complex than in the centralized functional organization, because the decentralized division structure creates formal barriers between individual businesses. This sometimes results in interdivisional competition that reduces the effectiveness of coordinating interdivisional activities.

Committees, task forces, or special project teams again can be used to provide important linkages between organizational units. For example, corporate-wide product development responsibility can be assigned to a committee of representatives from corporate and divisional R&D, marketing, and manufacturing. Or representatives from different units within a group can meet to explore the need for communication about, and coordination of, customer relations.

Organizations with a division structure typically have corporate staffs that reflect the functional structure in the divisions; they monitor, coordinate, and support divisional activities. Divisional companies emphasize both business management and functional expertise, typically using formal systems for strategy formulation, planning, resource allocation, and reward and control systems.

Flexibility is an important strength of a division structure. Divisions competing in stable, mature markets, where there is little environmental change and uncertainty, can have hierarchical functional structures that concentrate on efficient manufacturing and distribution operations. By contrast, a division operating in a growth market can be organized to react quickly to opportunities and market changes, ensuring that interaction among its groups will occur and timely decisions will be made.

A divisional organization's flexibility can, however, lead to problems. The ability to specialize—to tailor division structures to their environments—can make coordination difficult:

> A large industrial firm encountered problems of coordination when it defined three major groups: one a stable, mature business using a functional organization; another, a process-technology-based chemicals group that managed a product line; and the third, a multibusiness, multiplant, equipment-manufacturing organization. Top management recognized and accommodated the different structures of its groups, but no management systems or processes were in place to coordinate the three. The company is experiencing serious difficulties in managing the business as a whole, and management must either explore ways of providing this coordination or risk losing control.

Other problems in changing to a division structure concern the extent of such changes and of supporting changes in management processes:

> A large electronics instrument and computer-aided design equipment manufcturer reorganized some of its centralized functions into a hybrid division structure, due to its increasing numbers of

products and diversity of markets served. However, the firm's accounting system was not changed to provide the new divisions and their subunits with the information necessary to manage profits, for which newly hired subunit managers were now formally responsible.

These new managers had no way of learning how the organization's cost structure operated, and could not control rapidly escalating costs. They had not been given enough information (e.g., transfer prices) needed to make good decisions. Their expectations of subunit's decentralized responsibility had not been fulfilled either by the allocation of control over resources, or by the necessary changes in supporting accounting and reporting systems, i.e., management processes. It became clear that the old accounting system needed substantial modifications, and that reallocation of responsibilities in the hybrid structure had not gone far enough in some areas.

The message in these cases is clear: creating the appropriate structure for each division and the entire firm without considering other aspects of strategy implementation will almost certainly lead a company contemplating reorganization to a dead-end. It is vital to develop the coordinating and supporting management processes that help different types of divisions operate effectively together and in their own areas, as well.

The division structure is often most appropriate when the company serves multiple markets with multiple products. Through divisionalization the company can treat different businesses uniquely and react appropriately to the various segments of the marketplace. It is critical, however, that the structures be supported adequately by coordinating management processes tailored to the needs of the various kinds of businesses.

Holding Company Structure

In the 1960s the holding company structure came into widespread use in companies that were growing through mergers and acquisitions. A holding company is a collection of separate businesses—designated as divisions or subsidiaries—held together by a financial control system that measures performance and determines how resources are allocated (see Exhibit 3-4). Unlike divisional organizations, holding company conglomerates have small, specialized corporate staffs devoted almost exclusively to financial analysis. Corporate management and staff do not get involved in individual operations, but require division management to make all decisions, usually with the exception of financial performance decisions. Coordination among the divisions is much less formal than in other structures:

> Philip Morris was the first tobacco company to diversify. It had been a single-product business with a functional organization, and it wanted to move away from dependence on one product, to apply the company's marketing expertise in other areas, and use available cash for investment.
>
> Philip Morris implemented its diversification strategy by adopting the holding company structure. Its first acquisitions were packaging firms, which were acquired to hold its prices down compared with outside suppliers of these services. It then moved into a variety of unrelated businesses—shaving products, chewing gum, hospital supply, beer brewing, and others.

A holding company structure can present significant implementation barriers. For example, if the separate businesses are evaluated on the basis of their financial performance, compensation of managers must be based on the desired performance. If it is not, managers will not have proper incentives to perform. This is the same problem, on a larger scale, that the other structures encounter.

As companies move from a single business to multiple related businesses, and then to multiple unrelated and autonomous businesses, the organization's structure must change. Exhibit 3-5 shows the range of appropriate structures along the diversity-of-business dimension, ranging from centralized functional organization to holding company structures. In addition, the roles and activities given this dimension are spelled out. Thus the amount of diversity in the business as well as the strategy can be seen to influence the choice of organization structure.

Exhibit 3-4.   Holding Company Structure.

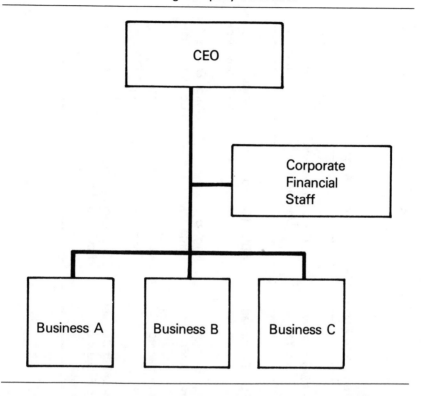

Matrix Structure

The essence of the matrix structure is that some of the key managers have two bosses who focus on two different dimensions (see Exhibit 3-6). The general manager continues to perform roles of power-balancing, decision-coordinating, and standard-setting. A matrix manager is in charge of either a function or a product. The "two-boss" manager responsible for a defined work package reports to both a functional manager and a product manager.

The matrix structure is generally used by businesses involving multiple products or families of products. Three criteria for using a matrix are that two or more modes (e.g., function, product, market, technology, geography) are equally or almost equally critical; a high degree of environmental change is accompanied by substantial amounts of information to be processed; and scarce resources are

Exhibit 3-5. Tailoring Organization Structure to Business Diversity and Strategy.

Operating Strategy	*Single Business*	*Multiple Businesses: Related*	*Multiple Businesses: Unrelated*	*Multiple Businesses: Unrelated and Autonomous*
Structure of Operations	Centralized Functional	SBUs (Divisional)	SBUs (Divisional)	Holding Company and Subsidiaries
Functional Units in SBUs	N.A.	Mfg. & Sales: Small Staff	Mfg. & Sales: Large Staff	Mfg. & Sales: Complete Staff
Degree of Centralization	Very Centralized	Decentralized	Very Decentralized	Virtual Autonomy
Role of Top Management	Operating Decisions	Operating Decisions and Review of Results	Goal Setting and Review of Results	Review of Financial Performance

shared within the company. The two modes of the matrix shown in Exhibit 3–6 are function and product.

The aerospace industry pioneered this structure because success could only be achieved by excellent technical performance and competent, effective project management. In manufacturing and service industries, companies have employed a matrix in international operations to focus both on products and on markets in individual countries.

Such dual specialization results in the need for complicated and demanding coordinating activities. Because the organization is focused in two directions simultaneously, the likelihood that conflicts will occur is high. In a high-technology engineering firm, for example, these conflicts center on sharing scarce, specialized technical resources across a number of programs. Functional managers and program directors are continually negotiating conflicting resource requirements.

Exhibit 3–6.   Matrix Structure.

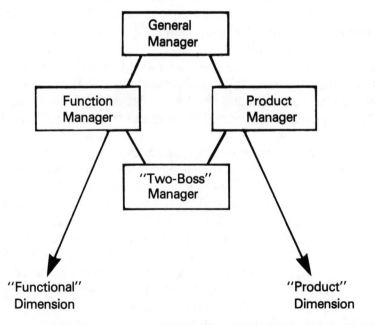

Adapted from Stanley M. Davis and Paul R. Lawrence, *Matrix* (Reading, Mass.: Addison-Wesley, 1977).

The need for coordination makes a matrix very difficult to use, particularly in organizations where people are not accustomed to complex communication. However, if this structure is used effectively, it can result in improved decisions, because the two dimensions critical to strategic success will be represented in most decisions:

> Digital Equipment Corporation, a manufacturer of minicomputers, is an example of a combination of a dominant-product business with a matrix structure. Digital, growing 30% per year twenty years after its start-up, meets all three criteria for using a matrix: engineering, manufacturing, and marketing are critical sectors; technology changes at a rapid pace, requiring a high level of information-processing; and resources are scarce.

The matrix structure, although relatively easy to design, is not easy to implement. It is a particularly difficult structure to use because managers have two bosses, one from each critical sector. The habits learned under the traditional single chain of commmand are hard to break. Managers must continually negotiate conflicts and maintain an institutional perspective at the middle levels of the organization.

In certain circumstances, however, the matrix structure is the best choice. If the willingness to communicate and resolve conflict does exist, a matrix allows decisions to be made lower in the organization where information originates and knowledge exists. Such willingness must be developed by continued training and reward, not dictated by management policy.

Citibank introduced matrix organization into its international business in order to focus on both geography and the global corporation market segment. This change, made in the early 1970s, was designed to increase the priority given to large international organizations, and it enabled Citibank to have a better understanding of the worldwide financial needs and activities of global corporations than the chief financial officers of these corporations themselves had. Matrix was a strategic weapon in gaining a competitive advantage with this important segment of the international market.

Determining just which structure is appropriate for a particular company requires a detailed understanding of the strategy, culture, human resources, and management processes. The last chapter of this book describes a methodology for diagnosing all of the elements necessary for effective strategic implementation; this methodology is useful in understanding the need for and direction of change in organization structure in the context of overall changes in the company.

CHOOSING THE APPROPRIATE STRUCTURE

Two concepts are useful in choosing among alternative ways of organizing the parts of an organization to complete tasks efficiently and to ensure overall effectiveness. These concepts—specialization and coordination—are explained in further detail below.

Specialization

There are relevant differences among aspects of an organization's external environment. These include accuracy of information, time span required for performance feedback, strategic variables to be planned for, and the nature and amount of interaction required. All of them affect the organization's structure (they also affect its management processes, human resources, and culture). These internal elements should fit the external environment and will have a strong influence on the type of structure needed.

In situations where information is certain, therefore, as in process technology manufacturing operations, a formal specialized structure is appropriate. In a research group, on the other hand, where information is uncertain and difficult to obtain, standardized roles and responsibilities and rigid reporting relationships can interfere with effective completion of creative tasks. A less formal specialized structure is more appropriate in this case.

If feedback about the success of an activity takes a long time, as in many research groups, the time orientation of the specialized organizational unit should also be long. In marketing, however, the time span is frequently shorter, because the unit must respond rapidly to changes in its environment or miss opportunities and suffer losses. The management processes that support the organization's structure can be designed to influence the time orientation of organizational units and individual members.

Differentiating tasks through specialization is one way to focus attention on particular strategic tasks important to the entire organization's performance. For example, a marketing organization must be oriented toward satisfying customers and meeting the needs of the market. People in marketing will see those needs as price, quality, and reliability, whereas a manufacturing group is more likely to view its key needs as unit cost, process technology, labor resources, and productivity.

The personal characteristics of the people in different subunits in an organization put boundaries on the capability of the subunits and the entire organization to take action. If a person who ignores detail were put in charge of complying with OSHA regulations, for instance, that activity might not be completed successfully. A research scientist who prefers to work alone may not be the ideal chairperson for a committee that meets frequently to set personnel policy. People must be able to perform the specialized tasks and conduct the relationships required by the external environment.

Coordination

The second important concept—coordination—is the coordination of all activities to achieve completion of the task. Typical approaches to achieving this coordination are through management committees, task forces, product managers, cross-functional policy-making groups, management information reports, and matrix organization structures.

The way to manage coordination depends on the degree of specialization an organization has in its units. Members of an organizational unit develop a perspective that reflects the important concerns of the group. Most strategies, however, require coordination of the activities of multiple groups. When a company's growth strategy includes the introduction of new product, for instance, the activities of marketing, manufacturing, and research must be coordinated very carefully. Coordination of new product introduction must accommodate the differences in specialized organizational structure. It must address the time, goal, and interpersonal orientations of the specialized activities and their representatives. The marketing person will be concerned with customer needs, product compatibility, special features, and price. Manufacturing will worry about the production process and its impact on the present manufacturing configuration. R&D will be oriented toward particular design features, the technology, and how to increase the firm's technical capabilities.

Conflict is the inevitable consequence of the need to differentiate the specialized activities and coordinate their integration within the organization. The degree of specialization within the organization determines the level of conflict and the amount and type of coordination that must occur to complete the task.

In summary, specialization is accomplished by designing the organization around the specific requirements of the environment and the tasks that the organization must manage, and by using structure and management processes to point the organization toward its strategic goals.

Coordination is accomplished by developing systems to coordinate various activities within the organization—planning, programming, budgeting, and rewarding—and adjusting the structure and management processes to achieve strategic objectives and coordination of all activities.

ORGANIZATION STRUCTURE: IN PERSPECTIVE

Most organizations' structures are hybrids—that is, they have elements drawn from more than one structural model. For example, a company may use a division structure for its major product lines, but structure the divisions to depend on common functional areas (manufacturing, R&D, sales). Another company may select a matrix structure as an overlay on a division structure to ensure greater communication among division managers.

The choice of a structure directly involves the choice of strategy. The first step in making a decision about structure is to understand what the selected strategy requires of the organization. A formal strategy should provide specific and detailed information on its effects on all aspects of the business. If the company defines its strategy as "continued growth in revenues and profits," for instance, the definition does not contain information about what is required of the organization's structure. But if the firm defines its strategy as "continued growth of 10%, with an emphasis on developing better market penetration and marketing programs through quality products," the strategy begins to focus on the need for appropriate structures to implement the strategy.

Managing the change from one type of organization to another is part of the strategy choice. Too often it is a separate decision, and the results of the strategy are not impressive:

One power-transmission components manufacturer had a traditional centralized functional organization for many years. Because of the increasing size of its manufacturing operations, it developed a quasi-divisional structure with profit-center responsibility for each of the divisions; the divisions had no control, however, over any of the sales or marketing staff. The group executive decided that profitability needed to be improved, and a third reorganization was considered that would focus the organization on markets.

The problems the group executive faced in moving the organization from one structure to the next were enormous. The traditional engineering-oriented staff did not have the appropriate experience in which to think about marketing; it did not have the right background even to develop the needed management systems.

As noted at the outset, strategy and organization are not separate. A plan for a change in organization must fit with the other elements of the framework that are affected. If change efforts are not coordinated, members of the organization will be sent signals that lead to confusion and ambiguity at a time when clear goals are needed. When a functional organization is in a position to diversify, for example, and responsibility for managing newly acquired businesses is put in the hands of the present functional heads, the old structure simply does not fit the new strategy. A division or holding company structure might, in this case, be more appropriate.

When structure does not fit with the organization's human resources—its people—the result may be significant resistance to change from managers who are critical to the organization's functioning. Some may even leave. For example, a matrix structure with a reward system based on individual performance sets the structure in conflict with the objectives of the matrix. In a matrix structure, by definition, the reward system must be designed to stimulate teamwork and cooperation.

When the established culture of an organization is entrepreneurial and favors individual performance, a matrix structure that encourages a team approach is not likely to succeed. This is often a problem in organizations with large R&D departments that must interact closely with the rest of the company. In some firms, therefore, pure research is sometimes held out of the matrix organization and allowed to function on its own to promote creative, individual performance.

The dilemma—to adjust structure or strategy—is not easily resolved. Ideally, a firm chooses a structure that fits with its strategy. When strategy is being formulated, the firm must view its structure as both a strength for—and a constraint on—the range of strategies possible. Conversely, when contemplating a change in an organization's structure, the fit with its strategy—as well as its people, its culture, and its management processes—must be carefully considered.

SELECTED REFERENCES

Beckhard, Richard, and Rueben T. Harris. *Organizational Transitions: Managing Complex Change*. Reading, Mass.: Addison-Wesley, 1977.

Davis, Stanley M., and Paul R. Lawrence. *Matrix*. Reading, Mass.: Addison-Wesley, 1973.

Galbraith, Jay R. *Designing Complex Organizations*. Reading, Mass.: Addison-Wesley, 1973.

_____ . *Organization Design*. Reading, Mass.: Addison-Wesley, 1977.

_____ , and Daniel A. Nathanson. *Strategy Implementation: The Role of Structure and Process*. St. Paul: West Publishing Co., 1978.

Greiner, Larry E. "Evolution and Revolution as Organization Grow." *Harvard Business Review* (July/August, 1972).

Kotter, John P. *Organizational Dynamics: Diagnosis and Intervention*. Reading, Mass.: Addison-Wesley, 1978.

_____ ; Leonard A. Schlesinger; and Vijay Sathe. *Organization*. Homewood, Ill.: Richard D. Irwin, 1979.

Lawrence, Paul R., and Jay W. Lorsch. *Developing Organizations: Diagnosis and Action*. Reading, Mass.: Addison-Wesley, 1969.

_____ . *Organization and Environment*. Boston: Division of Research, Harvard Business School, 1967.

Lorsch, Jay W., and John J. Morse. *Organizations and Their Members: A Contingency Approach*. New York: Harper & Row, 1974.

Rumelt, Richard P. *Strategy, Structure, and Economic Performance*. Boston: Division of Research, Harvard Business School, 1974.

4 HUMAN RESOURCES

Putting people in the right jobs at the right time without disrupting the organization is tough. We always seem to have the right people for last year's strategy.—VP, Human Resources, equipment manufacturer.

Formulating the most brilliant strategies and having the best organization structure will mean nothing unless there are people available with the necessary skills and desire to carry out the chosen strategy. As shown in Exhibit 4-1, human resources—people—make up a major element in the model used throughout this book.

How well an organization implements its strategy depends to a great extent on how much thought is given to the people needed to make the strategy work. The issues involved in fitting people to the tasks a given strategy dictates is the central focus of this chapter. Major questions to bear in mind include:

How should managers be selected to fill key slots?
How well have people adapted to strategic changes in the past?
How are managers developed for future needs?

MATCHING MANAGERS WITH STRATEGY

Ideally an organization is in a position to choose a strategy that can be implemented through its existing structure, management processes, culture, and human resources. As frequently noted throughout this book, when formulating strategy, an effective organization ex-

Exhibit 4–1. Implementing Strategy: Human Resources.

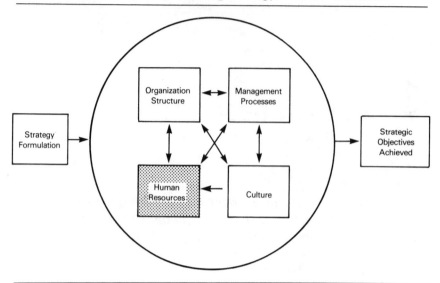

amines all of these elements to determine whether and how each element will strengthen or constrain contemplated strategic alternatives. The need for such analysis is nowhere more obvious than in the area of human resources.

The external environment very often requires a strategic change for which current managers are not fully equipped:

> A major money-center bank decided to embark on a program that emphasized selling of noncredit services to its customers. With the current squeeze on net interest margins, the turn to noninterest income was logical. The bankers had been traditionally deal-oriented and focused their efforts on lending activities. They were completely unprepared to redefine their roles as providers of a total package of financial services.

As shown in Exhibit 4–2, this type of situation can best be approached with a three-step process:

1. Define the business and the strategy.

Exhibit 4-2. Human Resources Decision Process.

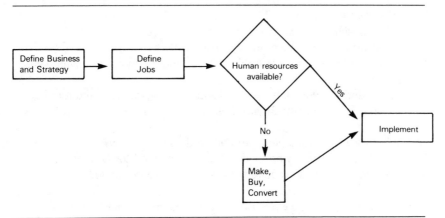

2.   Define the jobs that are necessary to implement the strategy, and calculate the rate and timing of change implied by the strategy.

3.   Determine, given the strategy, the human resource needs and the advisability of making, buying, or converting managers to carry out the strategy.

Each of these steps is addressed briefly below. To illustrate the reasoning involved, Exhibit 4-3 presents a series of questions that must be answered in the process. In reading the questions, a central point emerges—the human resource needs are determined by the special requirements of the strategy.

Defining the Business and the Strategy

As simple as it sounds, all organizations contemplating strategic change, and thus human resources changes, need to ask themselves, "What business are we in?" As noted previously, for instance, many major "oil companies" now consider themselves in the energy business rather than simply the oil business. To arrive at that definition, they followed the above question with two more: "What business do we want to be in?" and "What strategy will successfully take us there?"

Exhibit 4-3. Matching Managers and Strategy.

---

1.   What business are we in?*
2.   What business do we want to be in?*
3.   What strategy will successfully take us there?*
4.   What kind of changes will this strategy require in light of where we are now?
5.   What kinds of activities, skills, viewpoints, styles, etc., are required?
6.   In what specific respects are these new jobs different from previous jobs?
7.   Which existing managers can handle these jobs now?
8   To what extent is hiring or development needed to fill gaps?
9.   How soon do these required changes need to be made?

---

*The first three questions are generally analyzed in the strategy formulation phase.

This approach has a number of advantages. It assures an orientation toward future strategy and human resources rather than those of the past or present. It deals with what is needed for continued success rather than what has been successful in the past. In short, it stipulates that the firm must move ahead by building a management base that can best meet the challenges and opportunities the environment will present.

Having established that a particular strategic move is in the best interest of the organization, another question must be answered: "What kinds of changes will this strategy require in light of where we are today?" Top management must determine what new kinds of human resources actions are necessary to drive the company toward its strategic goals. Only by having a firm grasp on the answer to this question can the jobs involved be defined.

Job Definition

In defining the jobs required to implement a given strategy, it is necessary to determine the kinds of tasks involved, any special skills required, and what style or viewpoint will work most effectively. A change in strategy affects all elements of the organization, and a required change in structure, for example, might have significant implications for the type of manager needed. Basic profiles of the necessary managers—special expertise, decision levels, style—based on the requirements inherent in the chosen strategy, can then be established. These, in turn, can be translated into specific job descriptions.

The job descriptions thus flow from the strategy. The strategy creates a need for managers to carry out actions that require skills and abilities that are different from the demands of previous strategies. As this process is repeated for each SBU, what emerges is the degree to which the human resources of the firm must adapt or be adapted to match a particular strategy. Only by creating and effectively communicating accurate descriptions of these new jobs will the appropriate managers be sought, found, and put in position to implement the strategy.

Are Human Resources Available in Time?

The new job descriptions lead directly to the questions, "In what specific respects are these new jobs different from previous jobs?" and "Which managers can handle these jobs now?" The answers to these questions are critical, for they will expose specific gaps in the currently available base of managerial talent.

The final question in Exhibit 4–3—"How soon do these changes need to be made?"—and the degree of change the new strategy demands, are major factors in the determination of the approach to take in filling the "people" requirements of a new strategy. As shown in Exhibit 4–4, the amount of change and the timing requirements can be combined in a matrix format to illustrate what courses of action are open and most effective in given situations.

Type A—Slow Overhaul: Large Strategic Difference/Long Time for Change. A firm in the Type A position (see Exhibit 4–4) is faced with making a significant change in strategic direction, but the time pressure is not great. AT&T provides a good example:

> As widely reported in the business press, AT&T, which operated for years as a regulated monopoly, now must adjust to becoming a market-oriented firm. Undoubtedly AT&T will remain a telecommunications giant, but its products and service will begin to

Exhibit 4-4.   Four Types of Strategic Changes Dictating Different Approaches to Filling Human Resource Needs.

	Long — Timeframe for Change — Short	
Large — Difference from Previous Strategy — **Small**	*Type A: Slow Overhaul* Situation: The way the firm conducts business will change greatly, but over a long period of time.	*Type B: Rapid Overhaul* Situation: The change to an extremely different way of doing business must be undertaken quickly.
	Type C: Steady at the Helm Situation: The nature of the business is relatively predictable and stable. Most environmental change is transitory or evolving slowly.	*Type D: Full Speed Ahead* Situation: A very fluid and competitive environment, but one in which the firm's lines, resources, and tactics are frequently adjusted.

change to meet market demands and competitive threats. Its managers will be re-trained to meet the new marketing challenges, and other talent will be hired to fill new needs. Organization structure, culture, and reward systems will also, of necessity, change, and the change will be relatively slow and deliberate.

Type B—Rapid Overhaul: Large Strategic Difference/Short Time for Change.   Some firms face situations in which a very different strategy must be implemented quickly. The change in strategy may or may not have been anticipated in advance. The transition, as viewed by outsiders, is seen as relatively sudden:

For many years the Kresge Company was well known as a chain of neighborhood variety stores. Then, seemingly overnight, a chain of suburban discount stores named K-Mart appeared.

> In preparing for the change in its business, Kresge redesigned its systems and policies around a new store concept. It began to prepare managers to incorporate merchandising and control practices very different from those common to neighborhood variety stores. Many managers were hired from outside the firm; others were trained to fit with the new strategy.

Type C—Steady at the Helm: Small Strategic Difference/Long Time for Change. Many companies that have achieved maturity in their industries find that their basic operations are best managed with a steady hand. While some firms are sensitive to changes in the business environment, companies in this position are often able to weather many changes with relatively minor or slowly evolving responses:

> At 3-M, people are groomed in a process of assignments and reassignments to many levels of management. This gives them exposure to a variety of situations throughout the firm, and provides a steady stream of managers with a firm-wide, diverse perspective. New managerial needs are routinely identified, and special attention is given to supplying the new capabilities needed from within the firm.

Type D—Full Speed Ahead: Small Strategic Difference/Short Time for Change. For some firms the environment is in a constant state of change. Producers of consumer goods, for instance, pursue a strategy designed to maintain and add customers in the face of changing perceptions and new, competitive product offerings. In response, they must frequently modify their products, advertising, and merchandising, and while their strategy remains relatively constant, small changes must constantly be made within a short period of time:

> Procter & Gamble requires its product managers to make quick and constant adjustments to the positioning of products in the marketplace. The challenge of these jobs creates turnover of people at both the entry level and before rising to upper management. On-the-job training is intense. Intrinsically challenging job positions and a willingness to accept attrition of product managers are very important to the success of the P&G strategy.

Depending on where a particular strategy places a firm on the Exhibit 4-4 matrix, three basic methods are available for filling the managerial gaps the strategy creates: make, buy, and convert.

Filling Managerial Needs: Make, Buy, or Convert?

Borrowing a concept from production, missing human resource requirements can be *made* or *bought*. A third alternative—*convert*—is also available. Each of these techniques is defined briefly here and treated in more detail in following sections.

The Make *Approach.*   A *make* policy involves the routine development of a broad managerial base within the firm by grooming managers who can fulfill the requirements of a diverse range of strategic moves. This approach by definition requires long lead times and significant expense, in that managers are moved around in the organization to gain wide exposure and general experience in a number of areas. In this way the organization builds a management base that is prepared to handle most strategies the firm would consider implementing.

One major aspect of this approach is that such training also provides managers with a great deal of job mobility outside the firm. It also works best in relatively mature, stable industries that are unlikely to embark on disruptive new strategies. Furthermore, using a *make* approach has impacts on the organization's structure, management processes, and culture, for such an approach has far-reaching implications concerning how the organization operates. It is not, therefore, an approach that can be effectively embraced in the short term.

The Buy *Approach.*   "Buying" managers to fill specific needs a strategy generates is just what the term implies—managers who meet the requirements of the job descriptions are hired from the managerial pool that exists outside the firm. This has the great advantage of speed, but also has a number of drawbacks. For instance, from the standpoint of the firm's culture (see Chapter 2), a manager recruited from outside who fulfills the job description may not be able to accept—or be accepted in—the firm's culture. Such managers also command high salaries, and frequently the needed talent simply is not readily available. Thus, while a *buy* policy is often necessary in situations where new skills are needed immediately, it is not a panacea.

The Convert *Approach.* Given less time than required for a *make* policy, and enough time to avoid the pitfalls involved in "buying" people with the skills needed to fill the new jobs called for by the strategy, selected managers from the firm's current workforce can be retrained, or *converted*, to fill the managerial gaps the strategy creates. While apparently ideal on the surface, the convert approach also has drawbacks. Top management, for example, must be sure that the changes inherent in the new strategy can be assimilated by the organization—its structure, management processes, and especially here its culture—so that the conversion process in the human resources area will be accepted and thus effective.

Human Resource Capabilities

Most firms utilize a mixture of the make, buy, and convert options, frequently on an ad hoc basis. As shown in Exhibit 4–5, however, all of the options require the human resources function (such as Personnel or the Human Resources Department) to have the necessary capabilities to undertake them. Given the importance of timing in the decision process, planning is a major factor in the choices open to those who must make, buy, or convert. Effective firms have human resource functions that are prepared and capable of making the best decisions a particular strategy demands.

Exhibit 4–5 lists the capabilities any strong human resource function needs. Opposite each capability are listed special emphases demanded by each of the three major options. A dot next to a focal action signifies that it is of special importance (but not exclusively important) when opting for a particular policy.

As noted in the previous section, effectively defining jobs is the major link between strategy and people. As shown in Exhibit 4–5, this is true for all approaches. Defining jobs involves more than filling out forms. To be effective, the definition must clearly communicate the information necessary for decision-makers to fill the new jobs with the best people.

Job descriptions reflect inherent differences in the three approaches. When a *make* policy is pursued, for instance, the job description will

Exhibit 4-5. Three Basic Human Resource Policies and Their Associated Internal Human Resource Function Capabilities.

Human Resource Function Capability	"Make"	"Buy"	"Convert"
Job Definition	• Accent on behavior and tasks.	• Accent on objectives and boundaries.	• Define contrasts between old and new.
Manpower Forecasting	• Compare forecast mix with internal mix of managers.	Compare forecast with external availabilities and forecasts.	Compare forecast with internal mix of managers.
Career Path Planning	• Well-defined alternatives for advancement.	Very little required.	If already used, change path definitions. If not, wait until new paths are clear.
Job Rotations/Transfers	• Strongly emphasized.	Little emphasis.	• Carefully planned transfers.
Personnel Data Base	• Extensive information for tracking	Little except as related to hiring.	Sufficient information on experience and training to redeploy people.
Performance Review/Feedback	Regularly scheduled and formalized	• Frequent initial feedback on results and behavior.	• Especially frequent before and shortly after transition.
Promotion Reviews	Well-defined system.	Little formally.	Change criteria to fit new strategy and reevaluate.
Rewards	Small increments related to each success and personal progress.	Incentives for results. Avoid deferred compensation.	• Sharp contrast between rewards for new behavior and results vs. penalties for old behavior.

Recruiting/Screening and Outplacement	Done at lower levels (entry) with general criteria.	• Done at higher levels or with highly skilled recruiters and sharply defined criteria.	Little emphasis. Job-change counseling instead.
Organization Techniques	Standing committees with slowly changing memberships for development and visibility.	Task team for specific business problems and team-building.	Abolish old and create new committees and task forces.
External Education	Free time/tuition for business-related or personal improvement.	Very little.	Possibly for a few key people.
Internal Education	• Ongoing, on-the-job, non-intensive, staged (general education).	Familiarization with key aspects of the business (orientation).	• Intensive change programs aimed at each level to break old habits and views (tailored workshops).

• = Of particular importance to policy pursued.

stress what the manager should be learning by doing that particular job. It will define the tasks, skills, and behavior required not only for that job, but as preparation for other jobs, as well. In the case of a *buy approach, the job description will emphasize the objectives of the job and its boundaries or constraints. For a convert* policy, the skills and attitudes of current managers are clearly contrasted with those required by the new jobs.

Looking again at Exhibit 4–5 provides further evidence of this difference in focus for the three approaches. Some of the more critical capabilities involved in the make, buy, and convert options are discussed in more detail below.

The Make *Approach.* Keeping in mind that developing versatile managers with broad, general skills takes years, it becomes readily apparent that the ability to forecast manpower needs will be of central importance to planning specific development needs. Career path planning is also necesary to determine how people can and should move around and up in the organization. Job rotation, for example, is a way of providing development, but requires systematic planning so that one job experience builds on another.

In order to do both forecasting and career path planning, the firm will also need very reliable data by which to track people and to update plans and forecasts. Internally supplied education is also very important, for at each level in a person's development it is valuable to use training programs to introduce new concepts and skills appropriate to that level, and also to prepare for the next level or set of assignments.

The Buy *Approach.* Recruiting ready-made managers from outside, as the *buy* policy dictates, requires the firm to have a strong capability to provide immediate and frequent feedback on performance. Whether written or verbal, it is essential that the efforts of people new to the organization get quickly channeled into the most important aspects of their jobs, and that these people are told whether or not they are performing appropriately and well.

The ability to do excellent recruiting, however, is probably the most important capability for the *buy* policy. High levels of management should be directly involved with recruiting and with defining the jobs. Following this type of approach can also benefit from highly trained and experienced recruiters (both internal and external) in the screening and selection process.

The ability to do outplacement—helping managers find jobs in other firms—for those who no longer meet the needs of the firm is also important here. Some firms, in fact, have developed a very positive reputation even though they develop more excellent people than they need. They hire a large number of people into very demanding jobs where the job itself is an intensive learning experience. Although the firm retains only a small percentage of these people after a few years on the job, many other corporations with jobs requiring similar skills but in a less intense environment are eager to hire these departing managers.

The Convert *Approach.* Finally, for those companies choosing—and having time—to use current managers selected from their internal human resource base to pursue new objectives and strategies through a *convert* approach, the most important capabilities are again somewhat different from those for the other two policies. Carefully planned transfers, for example, are used to move people with skills and strengths no longer important in some parts of the firm to areas that now need them. In thinking through these transfers, consideration must also be given to the skills and strengths of managers that have not been fully utilized in current jobs.

Performance feedback is particularly important during and shortly after the job change occurs, so that managers are clear about what the accents are in the new setting. To reinforce the differences, particularly if many people are being asked to utilize a new viewpoint or behave in new ways, the rewards and penalties must underscore what is now considered acceptable and what is not.

Many firms have found that intensive, business-related education tailored to the specific needs of the new managers is also a driving force in the success of a conversion policy. Such education, often making heavy use of workshops, is aimed at helping managers see why the changes are necessary, what those changes imply, and how the changes require a particular different focus on their part.

Training Managers for New Jobs

Once the new managers have been selected—whether through the make, buy, or convert approaches—they frequently require training to make them effective in their new positions. In the *make* approach, this training has generally been done on the job, and tuition grants and time off to take courses providing overall management skills are frequently offered. Job training in this context is viewed as long-term and generalist.

Managers recruited to the firm through a *buy* policy are expected to possess the skills and other requirements stipulated in the job description. What training is necessary is therefore accomplished on an ad hoc, one-to-one basis with peers and superiors. Some firms do provide formal orientation seminars, but these are—like the approach itself—brief and intensive.

> **Exhibit 4-6.**   A Management Education Technique Used Effectively in a "Convert" Approach.

Background research
Interviews are conducted to understand: (1) the company's environment, strategy, structure, culture, and key systems; and (2) the managerial gaps that create the need for the program.

Objectives and theme
Senior management defines the program's objectives and the major issues to be addressed, and identifies the candidate business units. Based on an understanding of the company's desired strategic thrust and factors that may impede its successful execution, a fundamental organizing program concept is chosen. This concept serves as a unifying theme for selecting topics, faculty, and materials.

Detailed design
Specific program topics are identified. Faculty are selected on the basis of their functional and industry expertise and their effectiveness with groups of senior executives. Cases and other program materials are chosen, often supplemented by cases and illustrations drawn from the company itself.

Form teams
Teams are formed from each participating business unit, usually consisting of the business unit general manager and four to six key functional managers. Four or five business units are selected to participate in each offering of the program.

Frame issues
In conjunction with senior corporate management, one issue is identified for each business unit. The issue is a significant strategy-related problem or opportunity facing the business unit that must be resolved within the immediate

The *convert* approach, by contrast, is one that frequently demands specialized management training to bring managers in new positions up to speed. Upper management—and in turn the human resources function—is faced with the problem of finding programs that effectively fill the specific needs of these managers in a relatively short time.

One type of training program that is especially effective in this situation combines theory with practice (see Exhibit 4-6). Business school faculty are called in to give lectures and discuss business cases that relate directly to the issues the managers face in their new positions. Managers then break into teams for intensive workshop ses-

---

future. The issue is framed by the business unit team with the assistance of the consultant assigned to that team.

Logistical arrangements
Administrative and logistical arrangements are completed, such as site selection and assembly of program materials. Each offering of the program is usually four to six intensive days and is held off-site.

Conduct program
Each program consists of about 40 percent lectures and case discussions, normally each morning, to introduce participants to key concepts and tools. These sessions are conducted by distinguished professors, each a specialist in his field. The remaining 60 percent of the program, afternoons and evenings, consists of workshops during which each team seeks to resolve its issue. These sessions permit the teams to apply the concepts and tools learned each morning to gain progressively deeper understanding of their issues. The assigned consultant works full time with his team, acting as a facilitator or "coach." The workshops are intense experiences and are the real key to the program's success. Teams report progress to the entire group, culminating on the last day with presentations of action plans formulated to resolve their issues.

Follow-up
In most programs, a predetermined amount of consultant assistance is available to team members when they return to their jobs—to provide additional reinforcement, further refine the plan, involve managers who did not attend the program, and identify and remove barriers to the plan's implementation.

sions, where they work on a "live" issue that their new job presents. External facilitators, or "coaches," with expertise in attacking such issues, guide each team toward the best practical approaches to dealing effectively with these issues. When the initial program is over, the solutions worked out are put in practice on the job, and brief follow-up sessions assist with modifying or fine-tuning the approaches developed by the managers in the workshops and refined on the job.

> For the same money-center bank described earlier in this chapter, for example, a training program was developed in which the bankers (as well as trainees) were provided with casework and lectures on marketing theory. They also participated in workshops designed to begin development of written relationship plans for a customer's total worldwide needs. Each team was assigned a certain number of relationships, and each plan was criticized and modified by the program participants. As a result, participants went away from the training program with the basis for pursuing the relationship plans in an organized way.

Many firms have found that training methods such as these are extremely effective in their efforts to match their human resource needs with the special demands of a new strategy. One added dividend is that managers who are given the training they need are much more likely to "buy-in" to the new strategy, which is a major factor in moving a firm toward its chosen objectives.

HUMAN RESOURCES: IN PERSPECTIVE

Filling the human resource needs demanded by a new strategy is not a simple task. As with all the other elements in the implementing strategy model, decisions in the area of human resources are inextricably tied to the organization's structure, management processes, and culture. This is especially evident in a *make* approach, in which structure, process, and culture are also tuned to producing the bulk of the managerial talent the firm needs from within its own ranks.

Firms developing their own pool of talent over time must have the systems to forecast manpower needs well in advance. Career path planning is also important to the *make* policy in determining how people can and should move around and up in the organization. Job rotation requires careful analysis so that one job experience builds on another. To do forecasting and career path planning, a firm needs extensive data systems by which to track people and to update plans and forecasts.

A *buy* policy requires that an organization have a strong capability to provide frequent feedback on performance. The reward system must also send clear signals to these new managers. Top management has direct involvement in defining the jobs and with recruiting, which has overriding implications for the organization's structure and culture. Organizations using a *buy* policy must, furthermore, develop the capability to use trained and experienced recruiters, both internal and external, in the screening and selection process.

Finally, companies choosing a *convert* policy to fill the management needs created by a new strategy must maintain a broad perspective. Transfers, for example, which are used to match existing skills and strengths no longer important in some parts of the firm with jobs and businesses that need them now, must be carefully planned and acted upon systematically. Performance feedback is again important during and shortly after the job change to ensure that managers are clear about what the new focuses are in the new setting, and systems must be in place to communicate this feedback. To reinforce differences, particularly if many people are being asked to utilize a new viewpoint or behave in new ways, rewards and penalties must underscore what is considered acceptable and what is not, and these must fit with the culture of the organization.

Organizations that effectively manage their human resources begin with a strategy formulation process that recognizes the strengths and weaknesses of the current managerial base. When choosing a strategy that requires people with new skills, they select those people through techniques that assure a good match with the overall organization and its objectives. These firms then integrate the new people into the organization to create a smoothly functioning entity directed at achieving the firms' strategic objectives.

SELECTED REFERENCES

Beckhard, Richard, and Reuben T. Harris. *Organizational Transitions: Managing Complex Change.* Reading, Mass.: Addison-Wesley, 1977.

Burack, Elmer H., and James W. Walker. *Manpower Planning and Programming.* Boston: Allyn and Bacon, 1972.

Daltas, Arthur J., and Howard M. Schwartz. "Toward Human Resources Management." *Personnel Journal* (December 1976).

Kotter, John P.; Leonard A. Schlesinger; and Vijay Sathe. *Organization.* Homewood, Ill.: Richard D. Irwin, 1979.

Langer, Allen R. *The Personnel Function: Changing Objectives and Organization.* New York: The Conference Board, 1977.

Schein, Edgar H. *Career Dynamics: Matching Individual and Organizational Needs.* Reading, Mass.: Addison-Wesley, 1978.

5 MANAGEMENT PROCESSES: PLANNING

Oh yes, our company has a long-range planning process—a process full of paperwork, review sessions, more review sessions, and, finally, approval. But approval often comes just in time to begin the process all over again.—Marketing executive, automobile importer.

As illustrated in Exhibit 5-1, this is the first of four chapters dealing with management process. Management process is the set of tools management has available to implement strategy. These tools are related directly to the other elements in the model—organization structure, culture, and human resources—and must be dealt with in that context.

The major management processes that will be covered in the following chapters are planning, programming, budgeting, and rewards. Together, these elements make it possible for an organization to allocate resources when and where they will produce the best results, and to control performance in a way that drives the firm toward its strategic objectives.

This chapter examines the planning process, which is closely related to strategy formulation as described in Chapter 1. Planning and strategy formulation are, however, different in several ways:

- Strategy formulation *develops* an SBU's strategy, while planning *describes* the current SBU strategy to top management and provides the link to detailed programming and budgeting.

Exhibit 5-1. Implementing Strategy: Management
Process — PLANNING.

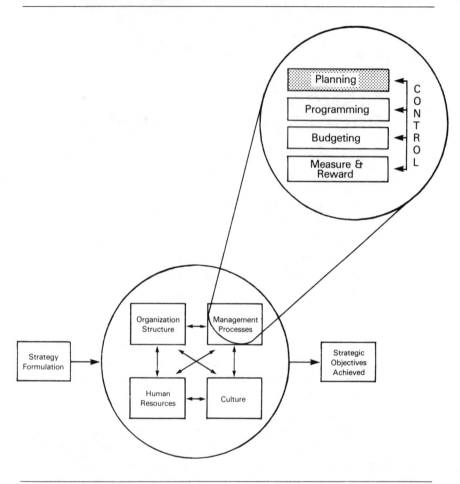

- Strategy formulation studies are done periodically when the need
  arises for a new strategy, while planning is done every year at the
  same time to communicate all current SBU strategies concurrently to management.
- Strategy formulation is typically an exhaustive analysis involving
  top management as well as many line and staff managers. Planning generally involves less effort and fewer people.
- Strategy formulation is done in reaction to or in anticipation of

changes in the environment. Planning profiles those changes and their impact on the strategy.

- Strategy formulation concentrates on SBU strategy, while planning pulls together SBU strategies and allows top management to develop corporate strategy and allocate scarce resources.

Planning, therefore, can be thought of as the communication of strategies to top management. The strategies may or may not have changed over the previous year, but the periodic nature of the process ensures that the strategies the various SBUs are pursuing are moving the firm in a rational way toward its overall strategic objectives.

CEOs of firms have a perspective on strategy and resource allocation questions that is different from that of their business unit managers. CEOs must be concerned with overall allocation of financial resources between business units as well as each business unit's strategy. Large, multibusiness companies take divergent approaches. Many firms—Beatrice and Textron are examples—stress the independence of operating divisions. Divisions must fund operations out of their own earnings and depreciation, which means profitable, cash-generating divisions are rewarded with the resources to pursue opportunities, and managers on the line and close to the business decide how to allocate funds.

Other companies—Texas Instruments, for example—are centralized allocators of resources among SBUs. Corporate management plays an active role in channeling funds from one business area to another. Centralized decisions can be used to redirect cash from mature businesses that generate it, but do not represent the most attractive alternative for reinvestment, toward divisions in fast-growth businesses that do not generate enough cash internally to fund all of their opportunities. Centralization can, however, create problems as remote management makes decisions without having a firm basis of business details.

Growth opportunities in apparently mature businesses can, for instance, be overlooked if they have been classified as cash-generators. Without regular reinvestment, pressures from evolutionary changes in technology and marketing may build to the point that a significant expenditure is necessary to defend competitiveness. Yet such expenditures may be difficult to get approved. Classification of a business as a harvest area, with its growth opportunities restricted, can also create serious managerial difficulties. There are many principles for managing businesses in high-growth modes, but very little attention is paid to the problems of running a business effectively with fixed or diminishing resources. It is hard to plan expenditures against a low and rigid ceiling, particularly during times of inflation. Every need that must be addressed means that some existing activity of equal or greater cost has to be discontinued. Motivation of competent and ambitious employees is very difficult in this situation.

The successful multidivisional company can create a management system that enables most decisions to be made at the operating level. Central corporate management still has the role, however, of channeling resources—particularly cash—among the corporate parts to the most attractive overall opportunities.

Useful questions to consider about the planning process include:

How is the planning process used as a decision-making tool?
What kind of communication results?
Does anything really change because of the planning process?
Do managers deepen their understanding of the business as a result of planning?

SOME PLANNING MISTAKES

The traditional approach to planning taken by many companies is tedious, time-consuming, and can be counterproductive. A case in point is a $1-billion diversified manufacturing company's approach. Its planning cycle begins in January, when preliminary long-term economic forecasts for operations are provided to the strategic business units, along with comments on the political and social environment.

Planning begins as business units develop their goals and business definitions. Capital expenditure requirements for the next three years are identified and submitted to corporate management. Progress against last year's plan is reviewed at the group and division levels, and new plans and investment projects are developed during the first quarter. Finally, long-term economic forecasts are compiled, and the five-year financial plan is updated.

At a spring planning meeting, the Planning Review Committee, consisting of the chief executive officer, president, executive vice president of finance, and several other operating and staff people, reviews the plans. Strategic business unit planning assumptions, progress against last year's plan, new strategies, and investments are evaluated. The five-year financial summary prepared by each strategic business unit is reviewed to determine the financial impact of proposed plans over the next five years.

Later in the year, the one-year operating plan is developed. It is an expansion of the first year of the five-year plan, and is the basis for the profit plan or budget.

The two critical mistakes this company is making are common:

1. Each and every SBU is treated equally in terms of depth of analysis. In the "real world," some SBUs require in-depth strategic analysis that cannot possibly be accomplished in the short time frame required. Other SBUs, because conditions have not changed, require little, if any, analysis.
2. A great deal of detailed data is prepared—so much that even with the huge expenditures of top management time, real understanding is impossible.

The planning movement that began in the 1970s has in many cases become a formality in which process has overtaken purpose: planning processes have come to discourage agreement among managers; plans for the future merely fill blanks on forms rather than communicate strategies; managers have learned the kinds of objectives and goal statements that are acceptable to senior management, and then make them, do what they want, and explain variances from the plan as "environmental changes." Even where planning provides an effective focus for strategic programs that will be developed, there is a tendency to misuse that focus: "We can't do that because it's not in the plan." Conversely, inappropriate programs are undertaken because "the plan says we do it this year." But planning, as defined in this chapter, can be used to gain agreement among managers and provide the focus for an organization's activities.

AN EFFECTIVE APPROACH TO PLANNING

Planning serves a dual purpose: to develop agreement between senior management and subordinates on the future actions of the company, and to provide a focus for programming and budgeting. But, as described earlier in Chapter 1, planning is *not* strategy formulation. Formulation concentrates on deciding where the SBUs should be going based on extensive analysis. Planning, in contrast, draws together at a single moment and summarizes all of the strategies developed in the recent past for the business or businesses of the company. Planning, then, provides management with information about progress of strategies and a plan of future actions. Once the individual summarized strategies are collected, management reviews them and makes any necessary modifications. These SBU strategies form the basis for corporate strategy and for the resultant broad-brush allocation of resources discussed in the introduction to this chapter.

Strategies are formulated whenever appropriate for a particular SBU, while all SBU strategies are summarized as plans and reviewed by top management during the regularly scheduled planning process. The more detailed processes of programming and budgeting will be described in subsequent chapters.

The planning process begins with the preparation of planning guidelines that summarize external and internal needs of strategic significance. These guidelines, which are prepared by top management, are discussed with each SBU manager and provide broad direction as the SBU manager begins to develop the plan. In addition, the prior year's strategic performance is reviewed and an initial discussion of SBU objectives takes place.

The *statement of objectives* emphasizes particular aspects of a corporation's posture, as shown in Exhibit 5-2. Summarizing the corporation's statement of objectives gives division managers guidance as they *begin planning* for their businesses, and it provides the *starting point* for revising these plans. At a minimum, the summary needs to include the company's intended policies for allocating resources

---

Exhibit 5-2. Example: Statement of Corporate Objectives.

---

1. Seek projects, internal or external, that rely on new applications rather than invention.
2. Develop a market orientation as opposed to product orientation.
3. Utilize borrowing power of subsidiaries to escape provisions of debentures and foreign investment regulations.
4. Demonstrate concern for the quality of life inside and outside the company.
5. Undertake acquisitions and joint ventures.

---

among its divisions. Such policies constitute a brief statement of strategy for the entire corporation.

At this point in the process the corporate office calls on each SBU manager to review the *strategic direction* of that SBU, specifying the scope of its activities and the objectives for the business as defined, and to prepare long-range plans, including a tentative set of goals for the coming year. Changes from the previously formulated strategy are presented. The manager may propose refinements to the strategic direction of the SBU that will contribute to achieving corporate objectives.

The *statement of strategic direction* includes a general statement of the programs to be developed to implement the refined strategy, including a discussion of implementation considerations and a rough estimate of the resources required. Detailed financial data are not included. Each SBU goal is evaluated in terms of the desired SBU strategy. For example, if a wholesale communications firm decides to enter the retail business, it is crucial to recognize that this will require a store inventory system.

An explicit statement of strategic direction serves two purposes: it increases the likelihood of agreement between top executives and the SBU manager about the scope of the SBU manager's activities, and it reduces the risk of repetitive efforts or competition among SBUs. In effect, it gives top management an opportunity to review all SBU strategies at one time.

Exhibit 5-3 provides an example of a statement of strategic direction. Note that this very brief summary statement captures all the critical information discussed by the SBU manager and top management during the planning process. Sections IV and V summarize the strategic progress last year and the expected environment in the next year. Sections I and II describe the charter and objectives of the SBU. Sections VI and VII detail the strategic objectives and resources required. And Section III shows how the strategic plan of the SBU fits the corporate strategy.

By mid-year, top management prepares a statement of corporate strategy and goals along with implementation needs and issues based on feedback from the SBUs. In some companies this statement sets ground rules about how resources are to be allocated among the SBUs, as well as a forecast of the results expected from each. In most cases, however, the statement is designed to provide feedback to the SBU managers about the corporate implications of the agreed-upon business unit strategies.

Exhibit 5–3.   Example: Statement of Strategic Direction—
Process Instrument Division Strategic Direction Paper.

I. Charter

To secure a significant and profitable position in the electrical and mechanical process instrument market with a selected portfolio of high-volume, low- and medium-priced transducers and gauges that complement and take advantage of the Corporation's reputation for economical and serviceable production equipment components.

II. Current Strategy and Objectives

In 1979 the division adopted a long-term price leader strategy to be accomplished through market consolidation, product line standardization, reduced service, cost control, pricing restraint, and increased indirect sales promotion.

The immediate objectives are to gain share by holding prices, while cutting costs to improve margins, and become the competitor to beat as the non-electronic instrumentation market settles toward maturity and possible overcapacity.

Limited development funds will be required to prolong the competitive life span of major established products and to develop the most cost-effective marketing programs, productivity improvements, and control systems.

III. Relationship of Strategy to Group and Corporate Objectives

The division's strategy is designed to ensure a secure and long-term cash-generating position in the mature nonelectronic part of the process control industry as long as it remains viable. The division is to provide funds as well as technical expertise, marketing, and other support to the growth divisions in the group.

Surplus development resources, such as the R&D department and system engineering functions, are being spun off to help form the new Electronic Control Systems Division, which is positioned to participate in the expected growth in the process control market.

IV. Progress against Milestones for Last Year

- Product line and market rationalizations are substantially complete and on schedule.
- The X-10 economy gauge line, now manufactured under license in Puerto Rico, was reintroduced last July with greater success and profit contribution than anticipated.
- Market share, as measured by shipments against AGIMA data, is at 21.2% for the year, 0.7% ahead of target, though total unit sales are up only 3%.

- Excluding planned media extensions, the SAE expense has been brought to within 1% of the target of 38% of sales.

V. Current Developments in Business and Environment

- With high interest costs, recession, and inflation, businesses have been deferring or canceling purchases of production equipment that use our products.
- Electronic instruments and digital control systems now dominate complex and close-tolerance applications. They are taking some mid-priced "low-tech" applications as prices fall, but have not yet encroached on our principal market.
- Two small competitors in our segment are getting out, although their facilities and trade names may be sold intact.
- Lower priced, good-quality foreign competitors are making slow but steady inroads, held back mostly by limited application engineering support and experience.
- Our strategy pits us directly against the foreign competitors on price and quality, with a small, residual advantage in service. However, with our present marketing mix, we are gaining share at a higher absolute rate but slightly slower relative rate.
- The circumstances and projections underlying the division strategy formulated early last year are being borne out.
- Increased sales and market share during an industry downturn confirm the viability of the basic strategy.

VI. Strategic Objectives and Milestones

- Complete engineering phase of P5-7 rationalization plan by end of second quarter.
- Examine feasibility of new matrix organization with technical representatives backing up sales force.
- Complete feasibility study on low-cost mechanical/LCD gauge line by May 5 (with Electronic Systems Division).
- Complete X-10 introduction west of Mississippi by end of second quarter.
- Complete phaseout of P-2 and P-10 by second quarter.
- Reach 24% market penetration by year-end, with unit sales increase of 10%.
- Bring SAE expense down to 37.5% of net sales for the year.
- Complete "New Look" packaging and campaign for June launch date.
- Develop and convert to integrated inventory and production control system by year-end.
- Have 12 all-distributor territories under zone structure by year-end.
- Hire 6 new sales territory managers with experience in mechanical gauges.

VII. Required Resources and Expected Performance

- The strategic objectives and milestones can be accomplished with internally generated funds while still showing positive earnings and cash flow.
- The division has a target EBIT of $2.75 million, before the corporate charge for this year; $3.4 million for the next year; and at least $4.8 million thereafter.
- Target ROCE will increase this year to 33%. The capital credit for facilities contributed to the new division will be in excess of capital required for replacement of minor production equipment. ROCE is expected to stay at 33% thereafter.
- The division is expected to absorb 71% of operating cash flow this year, for a surplus of $1.85 million; absorb approximately 60% next year, for a surplus of $2.6 million; and thereafter to generate at least a $3-million surplus per year.

The sum of SBU goals is likely to be inadequate to achieve the goals the corporate office has for the organization. To close this planning gap, corporate management can improve SBU performance by pressing for more aggressive strategies and more ambitious goals, diverting company resources into more promising businesses, or deciding that corporate goals are unrealistic and scaling them down.

As Vancil has convincingly argued in *Decentralization* (see references), corporate management is concerned with adjustments to the portfolio of goals. The first cycle of planning has the effect of providing an annual midcourse correction to the direction of the combined businesses. Momentum is a factor in the continued success of a diversified corporation, and a wise chief executive does not dissipate it needlessly. Rather, the executive supports the SBU managers, trying to make adjustments early enough to be nondisruptive and, at the same time, positively affect the corporation's position several years ahead.

The product of this periodic planning process is a shared understanding of and commitment to the corporation's progress toward the formulated strategy. The strategy is modified to include agreed-upon adjustments, and it forms the basis for the preparation of strategic programs as well as the budget.

PLANNING: IN PERSPECTIVE

With the risk of overemphasis, it must be repeated that planning is not strategy formulation. It does, however, allow top management to examine all SBU strategies in summary fashion at a single point in time. Planning provides top management with a tool with which to balance the corporate portfolio, communicate expectations, and provide SBU managers with a basis to begin programming and budgeting.

A desirable approach to planning emphasizes the statement of strategic direction to enhance communication in a simplified fashion. The approach helps to develop consensus about what the various parts of the company will be doing and what the overall corporate strategy will be.

A good plan considers the strategy as well as the human resources necessary to carry it out, the cultural strengths or impediments that could affect its achievement, and the fit with the organization's structure. The plan serves as a link to the other management processes where resources are allocated and controlled. Recognizing the linkages between planning and these other elements is a critical step toward moving the planning process from a futile exercise to an effective implementation tool.

SELECTED REFERENCES

Anthony, Robert N. *Planning and Control Systems: A Framework for Analysis.* Boston: Division of Research, Harvard Business School, 1965.
_____ , and J. Dearden. *Management Control Systems.* 4th ed. Homewood, Ill.: Richard D. Irwin, 1980.
Galbraith, Jay R. *Designing Complex Organizations.* Reading, Mass.: Addison-Wesley, 1973.
Lorange, Peter. *Corporate Planning: An Executive Viewpoint.* Englewood Cliffs, N.J.: Prentice-Hall, 1980.
_____ . *Implementation of Strategic Planning.* Englewood Cliffs, N.J.: Prentice-Hall, 1982.
_____ , and Richard F. Vancil. "How to Design a Strategic Planning System." *Harvard Business Review* (September/October, 1976).
_____ . *Strategic Planning Systems.* Englewood Cliffs, N.J.: Prentice-Hall, 1977.
Roush, Charles R., and Ben C. Ball. "Strategic Control Systems." *Managerial Planning* (November 1980).
Stonich, Paul J. "Formal Planning Pitfalls and How to Avoid Them." Parts I and II. *Management Review* (June and July, 1975).
Vancil, Richard F. *Decentralization: Managerial Ambiguity by Design.* Homewood, Ill.: Dow Jones-Irwin, 1979.
_____ , and Peter Lorange. "Strategic Planning in Diversified Companies." *Harvard Business Review* (January/February, 1975).

6 MANAGEMENT PROCESSES: PROGRAMMING

We spend a lot of time making strategy, but we can never seem to get the right amount of money behind the high-priority strategies.—Group Vice President, pharmaceutical company.

Programming is a second management process needed to keep the organization moving on its chosen strategic course (see Exhibit 6-1). In many companies, well-developed strategies and plans do not have as great a positive effect as they might because resources are not properly focused on achieving the strategy. Programming is a process that increases a strategy's chances for success by assuring that funds are allocated to activities that drive the strategy forward.

Several questions to bear in mind when reading this chapter are:

What is the link between strategies and the resources used to carry them out?

How are programs with a long-term payout encouraged?

Are funds allocated to different strategic business units based on their strategies and the programs needed to carry them out?

The emphasis in many companies is focused on both strategy formulation and short-term budgeting. But because the budget is sometimes not closely linked with strategies, resources can be allocated in a manner that stifles rather than promotes a firm's long-range strategies. Thus, although budgeting may be highly developed and provide

Exhibit 6-1.   Implementing Strategy: Management
Processes—PROGRAMMING.

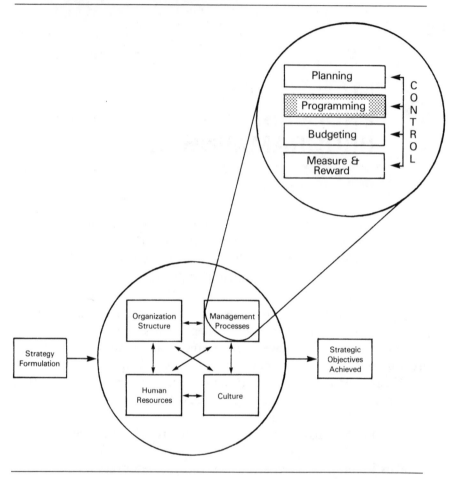

the information required to reach decisions about day-to-day operations and to set goals that must be achieved by taking specific actions, the resulting resource allocation often is short-term-oriented
and not designed explicitly to move the firm toward its strategic objectives.

For most companies, budgeting is accompanied by elaborate analysis, formal presentations, and major decisions. However, a resource
allocation system is needed that directs funds to those programs that

support the organization's strategy. This chapter discusses the need for programming and provides some insights into how Strategic Funds Programming can help an organization allocate its resources so that strategy is effectively implemented. Strategic Funds Programming (SFP) is an approach designed to enable companies to achieve their strategic goals by selecting and funding those programs with the highest potential impact on the future success of the business.

Many companies do not do a good job of matching levels of resource allocation with the different priorities their strategies demand:

A Fortune 100 company completed a thorough strategic analysis of its operations. It had split the company into strategic business units, analyzed alternative strategies for each SBU, and developed a corporate strategy and individual SBU strategies.

One of the SBUs, the drug division, with sales of approximately $200 million, had clear strategic goals: to gain market share and volume, to increase economies and thus force unit costs down, and to develop a position that would result in large cash payouts.

The drug division manager was pleased with his strategic goals because they offered him a great personal challenge. However, in the upcoming budget review he knew it would be difficult to argue for the funding increases required to implement the strategic goals.

This manager's frustration is common. As noted in Chapter 1, strategy formulation has become popular not only because it has given corporations a much clearer sense of where they are going, but also because it has enabled corporations to ensure a fit between the strategic goals of various divisions. But it is not enough to know where the corporation is going. Nor is it enough to have capital appropriation and budget processes. The gap between short-term operations and strategy formulation must be filled by a system that guides decisions about programs required to implement strategy.

Several types of problems commonly appear following the formulation of an explicit strategy, including: an excessive orientation to the present; an inappropriate organization structure; absence of explicit priorities; and a mature product orientation. These problems are, however, compounded when a link does not exist between the formulation of strategic goals and development of the annual company budget. If they are not recognized and dealt with in a formal programming process, carefully devised strategy becomes meaningless.

STRATEGIC FUNDS PROGRAMMING

One way to make strategy meaningful and action-oriented is to use the Strategic Funds Programming process. This section summarizes the basic steps involved in the process.

Definition of Strategic Funds and Baseline

A strategy is defined by a set of goals indicating what the SBU wants to accomplish. When strategic goals change, the strategy changes and the financial resources needed also change. Strategic funds tie strategic goals to the use of resources, thus enabling management to implement strategy through the appropriate use of those resources.

Three major components of strategic funds require the expenditure of cash, but are considered by accountants in different ways: plant and equipment expenditures, increases or decreases of working capital, and current expenses that will have a benefit to the corporation in the future but are charged to operations in the current year ("future" expenses or development expenses).

Accountants treat investment as an initial increase in net assets, and then as an annual cost (depreciation). They view increases in working capital as an increase in net assets without annual cost repercussions. And they treat development expenses as having an impact only on the current year's profits.

On the other hand, strategic funds can be viewed differently. Strategic funds are made up of three components: (1) investment in tangible assets (e.g., a new plant, tools, vehicles for distribution); (2) increases in working capital due to increases in sales, terms of trade, larger inventories, and loans to customers; and (3) current expenses that are over and above the needs of the existing business, such as an advertising campaign, large introductory discounts, or people for new product development.

These resources are strategic funds to the extent that they are used to change a strategy—that is, to achieve a new goal, to generate cash, or to expand the business. All of them require the use of cash, and all of them must be present to achieve goals. But from a discounted-cash-flow point of view, the net present value of strategic expenditures ignores accounting differences. The benefits are future cash streams, such as those resulting from more market share or larger margins. The costs are cash uses, some of which are one-time (new plant, for example), some gradual (such as increases in working capital), and some a mixture (advertising over one or more years, for instance). The common unit required for allocating strategic resources is strategic funds.

Cash items that are not strategic expenditures include: replacement investment such as that needed to maintain current capacity; current or existing working capital necessary to stay in the baseline business; and operating costs, both direct and overhead. To contrast with strategic funds, those required for ongoing operations can be called the *baseline.* All activities included in the baseline are part of the operating budget, not strategic funds. These baseline activities and the funds necessary to carry them out are appropriately handled in the budgeting process that is discussed in Chapter 7. The baseline includes revenues from existing products, related operating expenses, normal maintenance investment, as well as inflation-driven increases in working capital. Ongoing operations define the funds available for strategic deployment. Exhibit 6–2 provides some examples of the three types of strategic expenditures.

Identification and Analysis of Strategic Programs

Once the baseline and strategic funds have been established, strategic programs are identified and proposals put forth. Each business or SBU is analyzed in terms of strategic programs. Prime examples of strategic programs include new products, product modifications, process improvements, major research projects, advertising projects, and capital budgets.

For each program, specific strategic funds proposals are developed. The proposals require that objectives be set and that alternative ways be defined to meet objectives. In addition, each proposal describes how objectives can be met at minimum risk, the effects of not funding the proposal, and the risks of undertaking it.

Exhibit 6-2. Examples of the Three Categories of Strategic Funds.

Development Expense
- Advertising to introduce new product, reposition existing product.
- Introductory discounts, trade promotions.
- Free samples to stimulate first purchase.
- Developing distribution networks.
- Product development.
- Product R&D.
- Process R&D (e.g., for chemicals).
- Management systems of all types: Planning, Control, Compensation, etc.
- EDP programs (e.g., inventory control on-line reservations).
- Management development: Seminars, trainee programs, etc.
- Engineering studies: Cost-cutting, work flow, logistics, etc.

Plant and Equipment
- New capacity.
- New machinery and tools.
- Vehicles for distribution.
- Office space, warehouse space.

Working Capital
- Increases in sales: Inventories, receivables, etc.
- Larger stocks for better service.
- Loans to customers (e.g., for retooling).
- Financing the purchase (e.g., for automobiles).
- Better payments conditions.

An example illustrates how proposals for strategic funds are prepared:

> A European national railroad developed its strategy with detail for each functional area. The strategy was broken down into approximately 170 strategic programs. The board of directors stated overall objectives for each of these programs. As part of the strategy formulation, the board defined objectives for an accident-handling program in safety:
>
> - To improve the quality of technical and human resources devoted to repairing the track after an accident.

- To use capital investments to buy track-clearing equipment.
- To position salvage equipment so that it was not more than three hours away from any accident site.
- To educate salvage personnel in first aid.
- To publish operating procedures for accident-handling.

Proposals for each of the strategic programs were written in two parts. The first part was a diagnosis of the current position and a recommendation of specific goals and targets to be reached within five to ten years, and defined subprograms required to carry out the program. The second part dealt in detail with each subprogram, showing its results or milestones, activities, relationship to other programs, and costs and benefits.

For example, the proposal for accident-handling identified five subprograms: (1) development and publication of operating procedures; (2) light rescue vehicles; (3) heavy rescue vehicles; (4) human resources; and (5) control of the results of accident-handling.

In its first part, the proposal analyzed the total time required to clear the tracks. This showed that of 11½ hours total time (from accident to restoration of traffic), 2¼ hours were used to gather the rescue crews and prepare the equipment, 1½ hours were needed to drive the rescue vehicles, and 7¾ hours were given to clearing the tracks. In view of this information, the board's objective of reaching the accident's location in less than 3 hours became meaningless. To be able to do so for any point on the tracks would have required major investments, and transportation time was not the crucial element.

The manager responsible for the program proposed as specific goals a 50% reduction in preparation time (the fourth subprogram, training the crews to go faster) and a 25% reduction in clearing time (the third subprogram, buying some heavier equipment). The proposal was justified by its cost—lower than those required to meet the board's initial request; and by its benefits—shortening delays of passenger trains due to accidents, fewer cancellations of passenger trains, and less use of bus transportation to avoid the point of the accident.

The identification and analysis of strategic programs requires managers to think through what programs make sense, how they will carry them out, and the costs involved. This provides excellent data to the program manager and top management as they determine how strategic resources will be deployed.

Development of Criteria for Establishing Priorities

It is the general manager's job to develop a set of criteria for reviewing strategic funds proposals. The better the job is done in initial strategy formulation, the easier it is to develop criteria. For example, if the strategy for an SBU calls for maximizing its cash contribution to the corporation, then any cash-generating proposals would be favored over any proposals for new growth.

Several issues should be considered when developing criteria:

- The overall fit of each proposal to the strategy.
- The amount of risk that can be tolerated.
- The pattern of funding needs over several years.
- The mix of strategic funds used, with their financial leverage capabilities.

Establishing Priorities and Funding Programs

Setting priorities among programs in terms of funding involves several levels of review, approval, and consolidation. Managers should pass judgment on the need for each proposal, its risks, its fit with the criteria, and its chance for success.

Once the priorities are set, the programming is complete. The results, however, must be integrated with other management systems of the corporation. The recommended amount of funds should be added to the operating budget of the baseline in order to forecast next year's financial results.

Once the strategic funds programs have been approved and funded, the next phase is controlling the progress toward the initial strategic goal. This implies that the proposals have already specified a timetable, milestones, and other controllable and measurable activities.

Summary of the SFP Process

The process of strategic funds programming is illustrated in Exhibit 6-3. The major activities can be described in very simple terms, as follows:

1. *Identify strategic business units (SBUs)*. Many organizations are already organized by SBU. In the cases where they are not, an examination of products and markets must be conducted in order to focus the subsequent strategic analysis. From an external point of view, markets that are coherent and identified must be well defined. The internal organization and products need to be examined and fit within the marketplace. Common sense then dictates definition of the SBUs.

Exhibit 6-3.   Strategic Funds Programming Process.

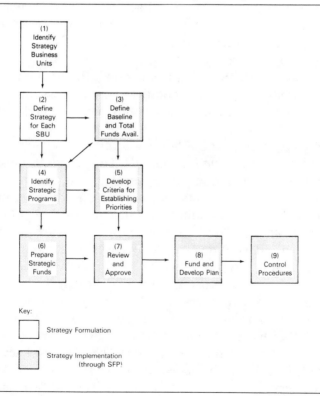

2. *Formulate a strategy for each SBU.* This is a prerequisite, but will not be discussed here because it is described in Chapter 1.

3. *Define the total strategic funds available for allocation over the next few years.* This requires first delineating the baseline—that is, the total funds generated and used by the ongoing operations. Defining the baseline is required for two reasons:

   a. All the activities included in the baseline are included in the operating budgeting process, not in SFP. This includes revenues from existing products, related operating expenses, and "normal" (maintenance) investment, as well as inflation-driven increases in working capital.

   b. The ongoing operations define the funds available for strategic deployment.

   Different companies may choose different definitions of baseline, depending upon the nature of their business and their degree of centralized control of strategic funds.

4. *Identify strategic programs.* Each SBU must then be further divided into smaller strategic programs. A program is smaller than an SBU, often with as little as $200,000 in strategic funds. The program may or may not be an organizational unit, but it will have a specific purpose or mission. Prime examples include new products, product modifications, process improvements, major research projects, advertising projects, and capital budgets.

5. *Develop criteria for establishing priorities.*

6. *Prepare strategic funds proposals.* The proposals must be both quantitative and qualitative, and express the results to be achieved in terms of market share or other market indicators, costs, risks, returns, and total funds use or generation.

7. *Review and approval of these proposals.* This process is not easy; several iterations are usually needed. Proposals often have to be redrafted or coordinated—and even new ones originated within the review process. To the extent that the initial strategy is sound and well understood, the process works more smoothly.

8. *Fund and develop plan.* At this point, the SFP process is complete, but its results must be integrated into the other management systems of the corporation. The recommended strategic funds level has to be added to the operating budget to make a final decision about next year's objectives and financial budget.

The end result of final approval will be a decision about what projects to fund, how to administer them, and how much to spend on them.

9. *Establish control procedures.* As the operating budget is controlled, so the strategic funds must be controlled. For this, each approved proposal has a built-in timetable, milestones, and other controllable activities.

Critical Issues

What to Include in the Baseline.   There are several issues in the programming process that need to be addressed in greater detail. The first revolves around the issue of baseline and strategic funds definitions. Different companies define baseline and strategic funds in widely different ways. One company's approach in defining a baseline requires a thorough evaluation of all the company's activities. Most activities are classified as essential for current operations (such as direct labor or raw material purchases) or for development purposes (such as new product research or a new plant). However, some activities are considered as partially supporting current operations and partially for development purposes.

Using this approach, some companies have been surprised to find that one-fourth to one-third of all the company's costs are future-oriented. Those costs should undergo the scrutiny of program analysis prior to inclusion within the final budget. Large savings can result from the rigorous analysis of various programs that have traditionally been approved based on their appearance rather than on their long-term value to the organization.

The following examples illustrate a variety of approaches:

> A high-technology, capital-intensive company, with many divisions and over $1 billion in sales, scrutinized all of its activities and segregated development expenses from current expenses. Upon review, major portions of traditional operating budgets—such as production scheduling, inventory control, shipping, and engineering—were found to be future-oriented. Quite a few of these activities were, it turned out, at odds with the company's

strategy and were discontinued. Today, the company uses a two-level budgeting process, with operating budgets being reviewed quickly at the division level. Development expense budgets are reviewed very closely at the corporate level.

A very large European chemical producer, with over fifty strategic business units in plastics, fibers, raw petrochemicals, intermediates, and paints, used strategic funds programming by defining baseline as the maintenance of its current tonnage production. As such, replacement investment was included in the baseline, but new plants and new processes were considered strategic programs. In this type of company, development expenses are relatively small and therefore can be ignored because investments in new capacity and working capital are overwhelming.

A different approach was taken by a very large consumer goods multinational. Baseline was defined—in every country and for every product group—as maintaining the current market share. In some countries and product groups, this meant considering a 10% growth rate as "business as usual." Strategic programs generally involved entry into new countries, diversification into related products, and initiation of a variety of programs to increase market share. Capital investment was relatively unimportant because of its low cost.

In addition to these examples, some generalizations need to be examined. A fast-growing company may be more interested in a wider definition of baseline, with strategic programs being reserved for true innovations. This requires very little groundwork and still allows identification, review, and control of the truly strategic decisions.

Determining Strategic Funds Availability. The establishment of the baseline precedes the determination of total strategic funds available. The determination of total strategic funds available requires an assessment of the availability of external funding in addition to the internal funds available derived from the baseline. A division of a European company provides an example of this analytical phase:

The division extracted and processed a raw material. In addition to selling the processed raw material outside the group, the product was also transferred to other divisions in the group for further downstream activities. The division controlled 100% of the market for the processed material (imports were negligible). Further, it exported the processed material to several foreign countries and had a reputation as a reliable and high-quality supplier. It had been able to use its market position to engage in "transit trade" (buying from one country and selling to others). The division's current extraction sites were maturing, which necessitated a major examination of the ways in which the division's strategic goals ("continue to satisfy the domestic market and maintain existing shares in the world market") could be achieved.

A variety of options for continuing production domestically were examined, including various levels of production ("produce at domestic demand levels, and produce for export as well") at various locations. Each of these options affected strategic funds availability because of differences in tax incentives and leverage capabilities. Additional alternatives for attaining the goal without domestic production were evaluated. Because of the accounting complexity, the competing demands of other divisions, and the interest of numerous political bodies, a strategic funds approach was invaluable in helping management determine how the company could achieve the division's strategic goal as well as realize other corporate strategic goals. Although the analysis of the specific issue was not unusual (the multiyear impacts, inflation impacts, and accounting conventions caused some difficulties), the approach was vital in assisting management to evaluate the trade-offs between the division's future and the corporation's future.

Process for Review, Approval, and Control. The third issue revolves around the methods by which companies review, approve, and control proposals. The methods differ by type of company. Companies that have uniform technology and a culture that emphasizes detailed central decision-making and control use a process much different from that used by organizations with diverse businesses, a decentralized culture, and less emphasis on detail:

A billion-dollar manufacturer of industrial equipment applies the approval and control process in a unique way. The company centrally reviews only major strategic proposals. These proposals are then monitored outside of the accounting system through a formal twice-yearly review with the planning committee. Formal accounting data is supplemented with estimates of expenditures and milestones. The smaller strategic programs are reviewed centrally as a group. The individual SBUs are responsible on a decentralized basis for the smaller programs and their control.

Such an approach is appropriate for this company because the company is diverse. Top management cannot possibly understand all the strategic implications in all the SBUs. In addition, the internal culture would not accept a detailed accounting-oriented system.

Approval and control are vitally important to strategic funds programming. It is necessary to check from time to time whether progress is being made toward the chosen objectives. In some cases it is possible to include intermediate control steps in the budget process—in other cases it is not. One simple and seemingly obvious example is the inclusion of market position in the budget and in monthly results. Too frequently, market position is excluded (because it is difficult to measure); where it is included, the intermediate targets are sometimes excluded because there has been no linkage. In other words, an effective form of control of strategic funds programs is to structure its output so that it can be included specifically in the budget process.

PROGRAMMING: IN PERSPECTIVE

For most companies with a strategic planning approach, there is a missing link between strategic goals and the budget. This connection can be made with Strategic Funds Programming.

If an organization develops a strategy and follows with a strategic funds programming process, it will have a set of future-oriented activities, *consistent with its strategy,* that have been funded. Future priorities will be ready for systematic examination, and priorities will balance potential gain against current funding for existing projects.

Programming is a valuable tool that provides cohesion among the management processes of planning, budgeting, rewarding, and control. In addition, if the programming process is designed properly, it will work effectively within the framework of the company's culture, organization structure, and human resources.

SELECTED REFERENCES

Novick, David. *Current Practice in Program Budgeting.* New York: Crane, Russak, 1973.

Shank, John K. "The Linkage between Planning and Budgeting Systems." In F.J. Aguilar, R.A. Howell, and R.F. Vancil, eds., *Formal Planning Systems.* Boston: Harvard Business School, 1970.

Stonich, Paul J. "How to Use Strategic Funds Programming." *Journal of Business Strategy* (Fall 1980).

_____ , and Carlos E. Zaragoza. "Strategic Funds Programming: The Missing Link in Corporate Planning." *Managerial Planning* (September/October 1980).

Vancil, Richard F. "Better Management of Corporate Development." *Harvard Business Review* (September/October, 1972).

7 MANAGEMENT PROCESSES: BUDGETING

Around here, budgeting has become a mechanical activity. We use last year's budget as a base for preparing next year's budget and add some fudge factor for contingencies. The problem really comes, though, when managers keep another budget that reflects their true intentions for the year.—Marketing director, automobile importer.

The third part of the management processes element in our model—budgeting—has a direct impact on how well a firm's strategy is implemented (see Exhibit 7-1). Broadly speaking, budgeting is the mechanism used to make final resource allocation decisions and to record them for subsequent measurement. In the budgeting process the dollars and people necessary to carry out all organizational tasks are decided and forecast. This is a key process in implementing strategy because it is very close to the action—the actual carrying out of the critical tasks necessary for the company to meet its strategic objectives.

Budgeting deals with allocating all resources—both those necessary to operate the business on a day-to-day basis and to carry out the strategic programs developed through the SFP process. As such, budgeting is a critical link in implementing strategy; without an appropriate budget it is unlikely that strategy will be implemented effectively. And budgeting is very closely interrelated to the organization

Exhibit 7-1.   Implementing Strategy: Management
Process—BUDGETING.

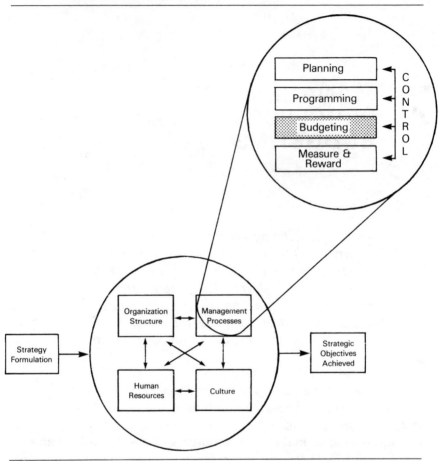

(who budgets?), the culture (what kind of process will be accepted?),
and the people (can they prepare good budgets?).

This chapter's focus is threefold. This first major section describes
what budgeting is meant to achieve. The second and third sections deal
with two very important parts of budgeting: capital budgeting and
overhead budgeting.[1] The section on overhead budgeting describes one
effective tool for resource allocation, Zero Base Budgeting.

[1]Management by Objectives systems (MBOs) are not discussed here, although these systems
are useful to plan individual actions and monitor results. Chapter 8 on Reward Systems
touches on MBO systems, and published materials on the subject are listed in the references
and bibliography.

Two of the major questions to consider in thinking about the budgeting process include:

How is budgeting linked to other management processes within the organization?
To what degree is budgeting restricted to number generation as opposed to results?

THE PURPOSE OF BUDGETING

As a management tool, budgeting is used to formally allocate the resources required to fund particular activities or functions in future periods. Exhibit 7-2 shows how budgeting translates the results of strategy formulation, planning, and Strategic Funds Programming into a concrete allocation of resources. Thus the budget is the fundamental tool used to translate all the strategic thinking and planning into action.

The budgeting process involves a variety and relatively large number of levels of executives in the organization. It usually requires

Exhibit 7-2. Budgeting Is a Resource Allocation Tool.

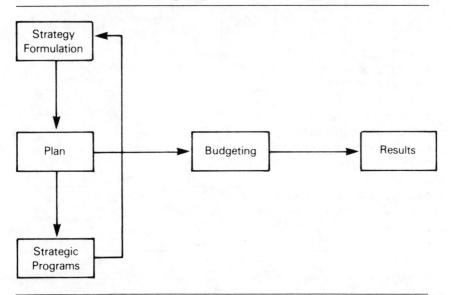

the participation of the chief executive officer, division managers, and functional managers. Top management generally requests that budgets be prepared within guidelines or limits; lower level managers prepare the details for the budgets, which are consolidated for review and approval by various levels of management. Exhibit 7-3 outlines in very simple terms the interaction between the levels of management during the budgeting process.

Budgeting is not, in most instances, an interesting activity for managers. The process takes considerable time, involves manipulation of numbers and frequent revisions, and is often unrelated to the day-to-day activities of the people who prepare the detail. Without a budget, however, a company will find itself troubled by financial inconsistencies, unfunded activities, and problems in trying to implement its strategy. Effective budgeting provides a link between the programming and the performance of a company's activities by specifically allocating resources to activities and tasks. By stipulating the amounts of money assigned to specific activities, it reflects management's pri-

Exhibit 7-3. Budgeting Decision Levels.

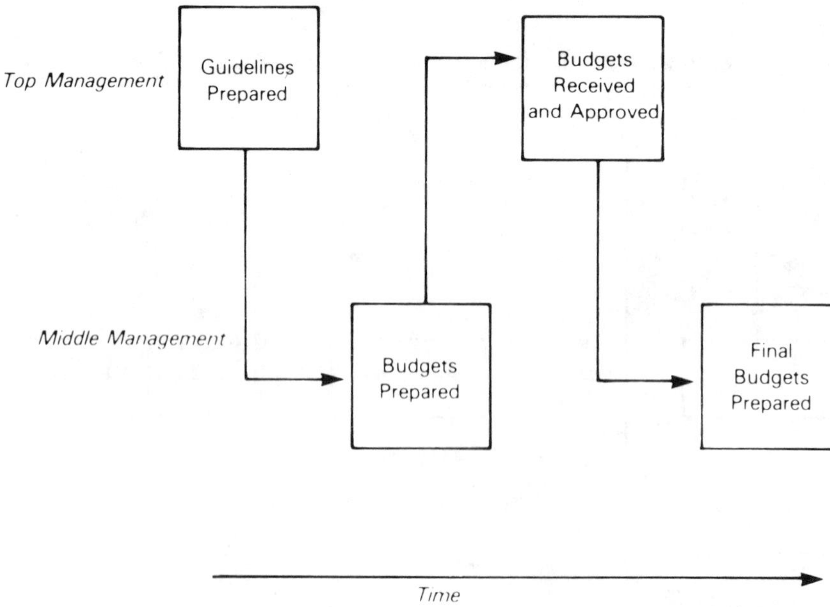

orities for the period in question with respect to sales forecasts, production, capital, and overhead expenses. Budgets for each area must therefore be prepared and coordinated through a process that ensures a coherent allocation plan.

Budgeting provides the data necessary for the measurement and control of functions and activities, and allows for an allocation system in which dollar expenditures focus on managerial priorities. Priorities can change as a result of a changed environment, and the budget needs to be flexible enough to allow resultant changes in spending plans.

An effective budgeting process is decision-oriented. The budget process is designed so that management can use it for making decisions, not merely for gathering information. Decisions need to be made about how resource allocation should be done to meet the objectives of the organization.

An effective budget is also action-oriented. Budgets tell management what actions or tactics will be taken during a given period. Strategy formulation points the direction for the company; strategic programming outlines key programs to be undertaken; and the budget defines the costs associated with carrying out the strategy and running the day-to-day operation. Both strategic and operational activities must be tied together if achievement of both long- and short-term objectives is to occur.

The budget process also provides a means to measure, reward, and control. The effectiveness of the budget is strengthened when it is a document against which reviews are conducted to ensure that managers have used their allocated dollars to achieve the plans they have presented and had approved.

To be effective, it is essential for a budgeting process to be understandable. Too often a multitude of forms is filled out to produce a myriad of reports in the name of budgeting. Data is not information, and a good budgeting process provides information that is understandable so that its users can make informed decisions.

A strong budgeting system is integrated with other systems to reflect a linkage between the strategic plan and the reward system. Financial aspects of the budget are only useful in the context of results produced by dollars spent, not by on-target performance in terms of the financial figures.

A corporate budget includes budgets for sales, production, capital, and overhead. The latter two, capital and overhead, are focal. The impact of capital expenditures is closely linked to long-term strategy and to the related strategic programs developed under a programming process. The overhead budget—all nondirect expenses—represents most of the controllable activities that affect implementation of the first year of a strategic plan. Sales and production budgets, while integral in calculating financial return, are of less concern to senior management because the budgets are operationally oriented.

Capital Budgeting

The capital budgeting process is discussed here from the point of view of making the process practical. Capital budgeting practice is in varying degrees built upon the body of theory developed in the last 15 years. The most accurate method of measuring return on investment potential, the most encompassing ways of incorporating risk in an analysis, the best framework for allocating scarce resources, the means of achieving an efficient portfolio of investments—all have been well developed in the literature. These techniques have been refined to meet the special circumstances of machine replacement, foreign investment, new product introduction, and other applications.

Unfortunately, much of this theory, particularly the elements that have been widely adopted in industry, is based on assumptions that have very severe practical limitations—limitations that are overlooked in adapting theory to practice.

Theory has tended to add rigidities and bureaucratic rituals to the capital budgeting process, leading to the following negative effects:

- Increase the time necessary to process an attractive idea.
- Reduce the output of worthwhile investment ideas.
- Lower the strategic quality of the total investment package.
- Increase the cost of processing an idea.
- Decrease the ability of management to review the real merits of an investment proposal.

An example of how one company approached capital budgeting is instructive—while pursuing noble objectives, it fell into a common trap:

A large multinational company that traditionally did not have a need for a capital budget developed such a system because of increased diversification activities where capital budgeting played a larger role. The company had outlined some of the parameters: the system was to use sophisticated techniques, risks were to be measured, and accurate economic analysis was to play a critical role.

Where did this company go wrong? The use of sophisticated techniques must be judicious. Analysis is costly and time-consuming, and use of the most theoretically pure analytical model may not be the most cost-effective for a particular company. Sophisticated techniques may increase the credibility of a capital proposal, but senior management usually does not need that much information to make a decision. Rather, when a proposal continues to look promising after reviews by various levels of management, the depth of the analysis is increased.

Many managers doubt the validity of the measures of risk commonly used in capital budgeting. Typically, measurement is done by taking expected value calculations and modifying the assessments by management preferences for risk-taking or risk-aversion. Such calculations should be done by experienced analysts, because there may be bias in the calculations based on what management wants to hear, and it is difficult to predict future events.

Economic analysis is usually done as an addendum to a capital project proposal and adds weight to the budget that is presented. Yet issues that are left unaddressed typically relate to a qualitative assessment of whether or not the products will sell. Marketing plans are often not attached and, without the questions that a market plan addresses (product definition, positioning, increasing purchaser awareness, distribution, etc.), chances of success for the capital project are low regardless of the quality of the economic analysis.

Procedures for evaluating capital expenditures are well documented. Three factors emerge as critical to ensuring that capital expenditures support the strategic direction of the company: (1) all levels of management must understand the purpose and methodology used in capital budgeting as the basis for obtaining support for the process; (2) integration of capital budgets into the overall planning process is essential, since major capital investments will affect manufacturing, marketing, and administrative areas in the company; and (3) the capital budgeting process will be dynamic if management participates in regular screenings to encourage the generation of ideas at all levels.

It is easy to lose sight of the purpose of a capital budgeting system. To be effective, the process has to be integrated with the other processes discussed in this book.

In most companies the capital budgeting process is a two-step process. First, an overall capital guideline, plan, or forecast is made. Then detailed analysis of individual projects is undertaken as described above. The first step should be integrated into the SFP process (see previous chapter). During SFP, general expenditure levels for capital should be spelled out and major programs requiring capital established. The final allocations for capital should be made during the budgeting process and at other times during the year as projects arise.

Capital budgeting, even though studied by "experts" in detail, is still an art. Great care must be taken to remain free of the trap of "showcase" analysis. No simple approach or series of tools will help the process succeed. What is needed is creative and thoughtful management.

Overhead Budgeting

Overhead budgets are often the source of headaches and much complaining within a company:

> The budget proposal is an annual event for this sales organization, and is a cause of anxiety. Depending on the state of the economy and the performance of the company, managers expect to lose, maintain, or increase their shares of available resources in the following year.
>
> The budget should fund the first year of the plan formulated earlier, yet the link is left undefined in this company. The tendency is to treat the budget, particularly the operating budget, as a mechanical process that occurs in late summer or early fall for the upcoming year. A common situation is one in which last year's budget managers are requested to update the numbers. It is presumed that the numbers support the strategy and plans that have been prepared and reviewed.

For example, whenever management dictates a percentage reduction in costs, the emphasis is on manipulating the various line-item expenditures to achieve the predetermined level, rather than on allocating resources to high-priority activities.

Furthermore, approval of the budget often involves substantial game-playing. Managers submit budgets without a request for new headcount, and thus appear to be staying within guidelines. Yet the budget contains dollars for using subcontractors or temporary help to augment the service level. Typically, no mechanism is available to control such behavior, particularly when the company controls by number of personnel, not dollars.

With the budget approved, actual performance versus the plan must be monitored and controlled. The common practice is to publish a monthly variance report so managers can compare actual numbers with those planned, and explain the difference. There is less emphasis on whether the dollars were well spent or whether the strategy is on target.

Zero Base Budgeting is one budgeting tool that assists the cost center managers, as well as senior management, in understanding the operation better, and allocates dollars to overhead activities and services that are of high priority. More important, since day-to-day activities affect progress toward achievement of strategy, management must be able to allocate resources to those activities that move the firm in the chosen strategic direction.

Zero Base Budgeting

Zero Base Budgeting (ZBB) is not an organization's "last-chance diet," nor is it an admission by top management that it has failed in its attempts to use "normal" tools. It is true that some organizations have turned to zero base in response to profit pressure resulting from changes in the marketplace as well as from neglectful management. But a significant number of successful organizations have seen zero base for what it really is: a process that brings together the analytical, communications, and general management tools that have previously been used in a less organized fashion. Management then uses these familiar tools to make a better plan and, based on the better plan, a better budget.

The use of the Zero Base Budgeting process in the private sector began as a well-managed company's innovative response to a constantly changing market environment.

> In the late 1960s, Texas Instruments (TI) found that its strategic planning process helped it develop effective new products to take advantage of new market opportunities. But TI also found that the same strategic planning process was not so helpful in reallocating resources from fading businesses, freeing these resources for new activities.
>
> Zero Base Budgeting was its response to this situation. The process was designed to help managers bring to bear the analytical and planning skills that were so successful in the balance of their planning process. Defining purpose, evaluation of alternatives, incremental cost-benefit analysis, setting priorities through a ranking process, and drawing the funding line were the good-sense management tools that were designed into their Zero Base Budgeting system.

Other companies facing a less dramatically dynamic environment have also realized value in zero base. Many companies have turned to zero base as a logical evolution of their management processes: a means of making the planning and budgeting systems congruent with the first year of their five-year plan.

Zero base is used by some firms to assure that rapid growth in sales is supported by controlled and coordinated growth in overhead expenses. Other companies have looked to the grass-roots nature of the process to generate innovative ideas and to focus attention—at all levels of the organization—on attempting to cure operating ills rather than treating their symptoms. Many have recognized that the process allows the organization to reallocate resources from existing, relatively low-priority activities to new and more important projects.

Zero base is a way for a new president or general manager to learn about the organization. The structure of the zero base system presents the details of the operation with the perspective of the group's priorities, and organizes these details according to the decisions that can be made about them. It tells a new general manager the relative importance of each item and what decisions are available concerning overhead activities.

Zero base also provides an approach to a company's need to control costs. For companies that may be seeking instead to improve their planning and budgeting systems, the use of zero base provides a link to their other management processes.

The Zero Base Budgeting Process

Exhibit 7–4 illustrates the major steps in the zero base process: (1) identification of decision units; (2) alternative and incremental analysis; (3) ranking; and (4) budget preparation. Each of these steps is discussed in more detail below.

Exhibit 7–4.   The Zero Base Budgeting Process.

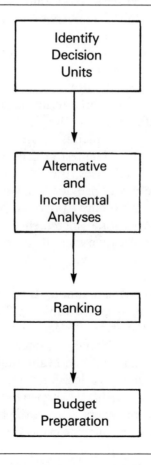

Identifying Decision Units.   The proper identification of decision units is the initial step in Zero Base Budgeting. In many cases a decision unit corresponds to the traditional cost center or activity center. Decision units may, however, include special projects or programs, activities that apply across the organization (for example, marketing, objects of expense, or services rendered). Once decision units have been identified, each one undergoes a careful analysis of the purpose of its functions and its current methods of operation, alternative ways of operating, and incremental costs/benefits. After managers review alternative ways of operating, including the current method, the manager suggests the most appropriate way to operate.

Alternative and Incremental Analysis.   Alternative analysis requires the decision unit manager to develop some optional ways of carrying out the function of his unit. The purpose of the alternative analysis is to open up the vistas of the decision unit manager and to provide higher levels of management with some alternative ways of getting the tasks accomplished. Examples of alternative ways to carry out functions are to *make* versus *buy,* to use mechanical means versus manpower means, or to develop alternative methodologies.

To begin incremental analysis, the decision unit manager determines, from a base of zero, which is the most important service need provided by his or her unit. Highest priority needs are the minimum increment of service. In all cases, the first increment requires lower expenditure than is currently provided and offers either a narrower range of services than is presently provided or a reduced quality or quantity of service. Additional increments of service and cost are developed with each successive increment containing those services that are next in order of priority.

Ranking.   Tradeoffs are made among the increments from various decision units in a process called ranking. The senior manager examines increments and analyses for each decision unit. Performance measures are included in each analysis, since they identify meaningful quantitative measures that assist in evaluating the effectiveness and efficiency of each increment. A decision is made on the basis of cost/ benefit analysis. The increments developed by decision unit managers and approved by their managers provide the basic information from which higher level managers allocate critical resources to high-priority activities. Once the allocation decisions have been made, detailed budgets are prepared.

The kind of detailed analysis that Zero Base Budgeting promotes is a model for the other budget components. Zero Base Budgeting requires that increments be structured in such a way that each represents a potential decision about whether or not to fund. The increments are also action-oriented, indicating what is going to be done at each level of service for the allocated dollar amount. The ranking process makes the process participative and understandable. Finally, with the dollar budget broken down into its various cost elements control of the budget is facilitated.

It should be noted here that there are significant differences between Strategic Funds Programming and budgeting. As noted in Chapter 6, programming focuses on future-oriented expenses, including capital and overhead expenditures that provide future benefits. The emphasis is on developing programs to support stated strategies. Budgeting, on the other hand, deals with operating expenses, and only at the time of budget consolidation does it include the future-oriented programs and expenditures developed in Strategic Funds Programming.

Preparation of the Budget.   The final budget is created from the capital, sales, production, programs, and overhead components. Each budget component is reviewed separately by top management and then viewed as a whole. A profit figure is arrived at by subtracting the variable cost and overhead budgets from the sales budget. At this point the detailed output of Strategic Funds Programming is integrated into the budget.

Management is then in a position to determine whether the profit calculated meets the profit goals set earlier in the planning cycle. If not, either the individual components must be modified, or the goal must be lowered or raised. The danger, of course, is that management will insist on modifications having a direct impact on the strategy, and still expect strategic objectives and profit goals to be met.

Once the final budget has been set, more than a variance check is necessary. A formal control process must be in place to test the validity of the budget. The approach in developing a control mechanism is twofold. The first is to ensure that during the preparation of the budget, the numbers are pressure-tested through a series of quality-control checks. Such checks help to ensure that managers and their superiors are in agreement as to order of magnitude and necessity.

The second step in the control process involves review. At least quarterly, if not more frequently, review sessions should be held to measure performance with the budget, not only in terms of dollar variances, but also in terms of what managers said they were going to do with the dollars allocated to them. This is why budgets must be action-oriented; in this way controlling performance is greatly facilitated.

BUDGETING: IN PERSPECTIVE

Budgeting is one of the more maligned management tasks, perhaps because of its traditional emphasis on form rather than substance. As an accounting task, budgeting can be a mechanical task. From a managerial viewpoint, however, budgeting is a tool that is used to make decisions about resource allocation—tradeoffs—whether among capital projects or programs or departments. These need to be made on the best available information the budgets can provide. For example, the capital budgeting system should bring out critical issues, such as "Who's going to take responsibility for personnel redeployment after the computer system is installed?" "How is that new product going to be sold?" Overhead budgets should be recreated from zero whenever it appears that overhead expenses are not supporting basic strategic direction. The way to become aware of this is to manage control of the budgets for variances in the numbers as well as the content.

The ability to implement strategy will greatly depend on whether sufficient resources are allocated to the chosen strategies. All too often, however, the hidden costs of adopting a new strategy are overlooked—a new organization structure or the need to train new staff. While not explicit line items in a budget, these costs should be explicitly recognized during the budgeting process in a descriptive (and, if possible, quantitative fashion). This will help ensure that the potential barriers to successful implementation of strategy will be fully recognized.

SELECTED REFERENCES

Bierman, Harold, Jr., and Seymour Smidt. *The Capital Budgeting Decision.* 5th ed. New York: Macmillan, 1980.

Hertz, David B. "Risk Analysis in Capital Investment." *Harvard Business Review* (January/February, 1964).

Lewellen, W.G. *Cost of Capital.* Belmont, Calif.: Wadsworth, 1969.

Odiorne, George S. *Management by Objectives: A System of Managerial Leadership.* Belmont, Calif.: Pitman, 1965.

Pyhrr, Peter A. *Zero-Base Budgeting.* New York: Wiley, 1973.

Stonich, Paul J. "Budgets and Budget Preparation." In *Encyclopedia of Professional Management.* New York: McGraw-Hill, 1979.

_____ . *Zero-Base Planning and Budgeting: Improved Cost Control and Resource Allocation.* Homewood, Ill.: Dow Jones-Irwin, 1977.

_____ . "Zero Base Planning and Budgeting: A New Approach." *Today's Manager* (May/June, 1976).

_____ . "Zero Base Planning: A Management Tool." *Managerial Planning* (July/August, 1976).

_____ , and Robert F. Vandell. "Capital Budgeting: Theory or Results?" *Financial Executive* (August 1973).

8 MANAGEMENT PROCESSES: MEASUREMENT AND REWARD SYSTEMS

Even though we are paid based on current performance, I still try to do what's best for the division over the long haul. But it's hard to ignore the impact on my paycheck.—Division manager, multinational chemical company.

The final part of the management processes area covered in this book concerns measuring and rewarding (see Exhibit 8-1). Measurement and reward systems involve considerations well beyond salary and benefit packages required to attract and keep people of the caliber needed to implement an organization's chosen strategy. Effective systems also *motivate* the organization's people to work toward the overall objectives established during strategy formulation and being articulated through the planning, programming, and budgeting processes discussed in earlier chapters.

Measurement and reward systems send tangible signals to the organization's people about their performance. Sending one message through an explicit strategy statement and a conflicting one through the measurement or reward system can only cause confusion and suboptimal results. Changing the reward system can be a powerful tool in altering the behavior of people in an organization. Because of the very personal implications of changes in rewards and reward systems, however, the area should be approached with care. The delicate nature

Exhibit 8-1.   Implementing Strategy: Management
Process—MEASUREMENT AND REWARD SYSTEMS.

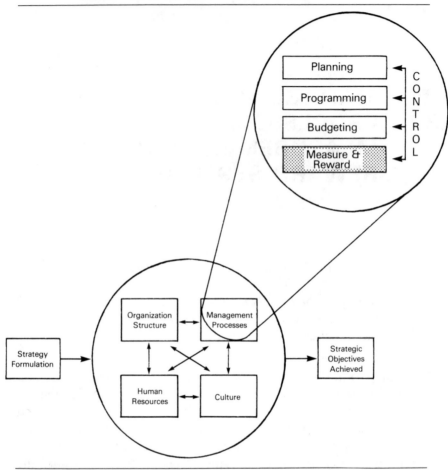

of the subject area is such that changes must often be tactfully planned. Reward systems can be extremely important in bringing to fruition the analysis and energy that have have been invested to make changes, in that they can be a significant force in moving the organization toward implementing the desired strategic change.

Central questions to keep in mind when examining the effectiveness of a particular reward system include:

How do the measurement and reward systems fit with strategy, structure, human resources, culture, and other management processes?

Do the measurement and reward systems provide incentives to accomplish both the long-term strategies and short-term objectives of the organization?

What incentives are available to all divisional or strategic business unit managers?

ALIGNING MEASUREMENT AND ORGANIZATION

Aligning measurement systems with other parts of a company's strategy and organization is a creative process that is frequently overlooked. Many companies simply use profit centers as their primary method of measuring SBU and management performance. This common method is followed on the assumption that most managers like to have a feeling of total responsibility and bottom-line contribution. However, such a simplistic approach to performance measurement fails to recognize the opportunity to use measurement as a creative method for aligning a company's strategy and organization.

Exhibit 8-2 illustrates how measurement systems can be aligned with organization structure and strategy. Companies following a centralized, often functional, organizational philosophy frequently use functional measurements for performance. At the other extreme, decentralized companies, such as holding companies, often use return on equity (ROE) as the primary method of performance measurement. As shown in the exhibit, the use of profit center measurement is frequently aligned with divisional organization. However, such alignment is not automatically desirable and, too frequently, companies adopt profit center measurement even though they are not using a decentralized, divisional-type of organizational format.

The diamonds in the Exhibit 8-2 mark changes in the position of a large money center bank as it worked to align its organization philosophy, measurement methodology, and business strategy:

> During the 1970s this money center commercial bank followed a traditional approach to organization and measurement by using divisions and return on assets as its primary focus. As commercial banking evolved as a result of high inflation rates and in-

creased internationalization of the banking business, the bank introduced a number of changes in its organization and measurement in order to improve the alignment of the bank with its environment. Matrix organization was introduced in order to recognize the dual nature of many aspects of the banking business. For example, funds management within branches was placed in a matrix, reporting to both the local branch manager and a centralized funds management organization. International commercial banking was also matrixed, with some loan officers reporting to both the local branch management and a centralized world corporation management group.

This shift in organization paralleled the company's strategic decisions to emphasize its services to large global corporations and to improve its control of the funding or treasury side of the bank. The move toward matrix organization was in effect a move toward more centralized control of the bank's activities.

Paralleling this change in organization, the bank changed its measurement system to reduce the dependence on return on assets and used a contribution form of measurement. The bank also double-counted the contribution coming from those operations operating in a matrix, thereby further reducing the bottom-line orientation previously used in the bank. The purpose of this measurement change was to reinforce the cooperation required by the more centralized form of organization being used by the bank. In this example, measurement philosophy was directly aligned with organizational philosophy in order to implement the strategy intended by the bank.

In many situations, implementing strategy involves a misalignment of organizational and measurement philosophies. For example, a company may be driven toward decentralization by the need to spread its operations across a broad geographic area. The independence created by physical separation frequently creates a drive for decentralized forms of organization and complementary forms of measurement. However, many organizations seeking to maintain a firmwide approach to their products or services, striving for overall efficiency and effectiveness as opposed to automatically opting for decentralized responsiveness, consciously choose a mismatch of organizational and measurement philosophies to accomplish this purpose:

Exhibit 8-2.   Divisional Measurement Options.

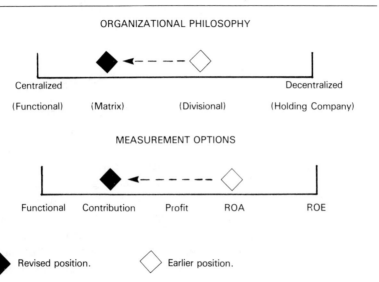

ORGANIZATIONAL PHILOSOPHY

Centralized   Decentralized

(Functional)   (Matrix)   (Divisional)   (Holding Company)

MEASUREMENT OPTIONS

Functional   Contribution   Profit   ROA   ROE

◆ Revised position.   ◇ Earlier position.

A large consulting firm operating in over twenty offices around the world chooses to use a single profit center for measuring performance in the firm. In spite of the fact that in terms of organizational design each of its offices is accorded a degree of independence approaching that of divisions, this firm does not measure profit at the office level. Rather, use is made of functional forms of measurement, such as overhead control, salary control, firmwide utilization and productivity measures, and revenue measures. The firm deliberately does not bring these functional measurements together to create a profit calculation for each office in the organization.

This mismatch between organizational and measurement philosophy is explicitly designed to recognize the realities of geography through organizational form, and to offset this reality with a measurement philosophy that requires a firmwide view. In this manner the firm is able to maintain consistency in practice across the firm, to force individual offices to work together toward the common good of the firm, and to strive for firmwide benefits and economies that would inevitably be lost by a measurement philosophy that was as decentralized as the firm's organizational philosophy.

Measurement philosophy is a creative opportunity that can be used to complement or counterbalance what a company is doing with its organization as it seeks to move in a new strategic direction.

SHORT-RUN VS. LONG-RUN PERSPECTIVE

A second area of particular concern in designing measurement and reward systems is success in the short run versus the achievement of long-range strategies. The short-term orientation of managers is a problem many companies face, and too frequently managers are rewarded on the basis of reaching short-term goals. Successful top managers know what they do well, and what actions have led to their success. Most often they have succeeded because the performance of their business units has been outstanding in the short term.

Executive compensation for performance as measured by earnings is usually tied to a bonus system. Bonuses generally are determined at the division level on the basis of absolute division profits, division profit improvement, profits compared with the company's or division's industry, or achievement of a profit plan.

Measurements based on these goals have a strong influence on division performance. One influence is the bonus itself, which can, in an excellent year, greatly increase an executive's pay. Another is that such measurements call attention to what leads to success and greater responsibility within the organization.

A manager aspiring to promotion reads the signals and performs accordingly in his or her decision-making role. That manager is receptive to low-risk projects that will show up on one of the measurement indices within the next few years. To suggest that the good manager will automatically consider the long-term well-being of the company and, at the same time, achieve conflicting short-run goals is naive. Short-run goals will prevail.

Within the conceptual framework of strategy implementation, then, reward systems are critical. People respond to rewards; the establishment of a reward system that fits the strategy can significantly improve the performance of an organization, and cannot be left to compensation specialists alone. The chief executive officer who operates with a well-designed reward system sees other management processes work more effectively, as well:

A large manufacturing company recently completed a rigorous planning process that went far beyond what most companies attempt. In an effort to tie long-term strategy to operations, an executive committee identified programs having long-term benefits and funded those programs on a priority basis. However, the expected surge of managerial enthusiasm in support of the future-oriented programs failed to appear. The reason for the absence of enthusiasm was ultimately uncovered: the reward system continued to reinforce attainment of short-term goals.

The firm's approach for bridging this strategy/results gulf was creative. After categorizing each of its strategic business units as "high growth," "medium growth," or "maintenance," it developed a measurement system unique to the desired strategy and growth for each unit.

The new weighted-factor approach (see below) measured the performance of each unit against the strategic goals of that unit. High-growth SBUs were measured in terms of market share, sales growth, designated future payoff, and progress of several future-oriented strategic projects. Low-growth SBUs were measured in terms of their cash-generating ability.

Just one year after initiating the new measurement and reward system, management behavior began to change. There was a noticeable increase in enthusiasm for the strategy formulation, planning, and programming processes, resulting in improved implementation.

Several approaches are available to help match rewards with explicit strategic goals, including weighted-factor, long-term evaluation, strategic funds, and combined approaches.

Weighted-Factor Approach

The weighted-factor approach used by the manufacturing company described above called for developing a measurement system that fit the behavior required of each strategic business unit to achieve its strategic goals. Figure 8–3 illustrates how performance measurement factors such as ROA, cash flow, strategic funds programs, and increases in market share are weighted according to the importance of

Exhibit 8-3. A Weighted-Factor Approach Used to Reward Achievement of Strategic Goals.

SBU Category	Factor	Weight
High Growth	Return on Assets	10%
	Cash Flow	0%
	Strategic Funds Programs	45%
	Market Share Increase	45%
		100%
Medium Growth	Return on Assets	25%
	Cash Flow	25%
	Strategic Funds Programs	25%
	Market Share Increase	25%
		100%
Low Growth	Return on Assets	50%
	Cash Flow	50%
	Strategic Funds Programs	0%
	Market Share Increase	0%
		100%

each factor in achieving the SBU's desired performance. SBUs were categorized as high-, medium-, or low-growth.

This weighting of performance measurements reflects the generally accepted idea that funds should be invested in SBUs with high growth opportunity. Conversely, where it has been deemed that there is little opportunity for growth, cash flow and return on assets are weighted more heavily. This weighted-factor approach can be fine-tuned to reflect each individual strategy by using additional points such as target market share, productivity levels, product quality measures, product development measures, and personnel development measures. These measurements form the basis for determining appropriate rewards.

Long-Term Evaluation Approach

Another way of explicitly motivating managers toward a future orientation is to use long-term evaluation that compensates managers for achieving set goals over a multiyear period. This approach usually involves awarding deferred stock, based on attaining an earnings growth target over a multiyear period. Alternatively, it can be designed so that payments of bonuses are reinvested in the business, and growth of the reinvested bonuses is contingent on future corporate and unit performance. Currently about 15% of companies with sales over $500 million have long-term income programs that compensate managers with some sort of deferred stock to achieve set goals over a multiyear period.

Strategic Funds Approach

A strategic funds approach is a third way to improve the linkage between the short term and the long term. This approach encourages executives to consider certain developmental expenses apart from current operations. Exhibit 8-4 shows an income statement somewhat different from that which accountants require for outside reporting purposes. Note that the manager is measured on two bases. The top part of the income statement is familiar in that it shows sales, cost of sales, gross margin, operating SG&A, and operating performance.

Unique in this statement is that strategic funds, conventionally included in the SG&A account, are separated out below operating ROS. The manager is given an incentive to invest strategic funds in the future and is able to determine how much is invested in the future of the business. The statement indicates pretax profitability both before and after strategic funds.

Exhibit 8-4. SBU P&L Illustrating Segregation of Strategic Funds.

Sales	$12,300,000
Cost of Sales	− 6,900,000
Gross Margin	$ 5,400,000
Operating G&A	− 3,700,000
Operating SG&A	$ 1,700,000, or 33%
Strategic Funds	− 1,000,000
Pre-tax Profit	$ 700,000, or 13.6%

This approach differentiates between those monies spent on future-oriented activities and those expended on current activities. Managers who follow their natural inclination to manage to the "bottom line" are able to do so if operating ROA is considered the bottom line. Thus current operations of the company need not be short-changed and, more importantly, future investments through strategic funds are encouraged.

Combined Approach

An effective way to achieve the strategic results desired through a reward system is to combine the weighted-factor, long-term evaluation, and strategic funds approaches:

1. Segregate future-oriented strategic funds from short-term funds, list them, and report them as in the strategic funds approach.
2. Develop a weighted-factor chart for each strategic business unit, including return on assets, cash flow, strategic funds programs, market share increase, and others. (Specific factors taken into account depend on the strategy of the particular business unit.)
3. Measure performance on three bases: the bottom line in the strategic funds approach; the weighted factors; and long-term evaluation of the corporation's and SBU's performances.

The relative weights that can be assigned to each of these in a combined approach will vary from SBU to SBU and from company to company depending upon its business environment and the culture of the organization.

MEASUREMENT AND REWARD
SYSTEMS: IN PERSPECTIVE

Performance measurement systems can be used effectively to drive strategy by aligning them with the organization's structure. Simply following profit center measurement techniques can produce suboptimal results. Firms that view the choice of how to measure performance as a creative opportunity generally gain significant benefits through successfully implemented strategies.

Reward systems can be designed to motivate both short-term and long-term performance. The company that rewards exclusively on the basis of today's bottom line may well be hindering the achievement of its long-term strategic goals. Several types of reward systems work to support strategy with management incentives without sacrificing short-term performance: weighted factor, long-term evaluation, strategic funds, and a combined approach that utilizes features of the other three.

The reward system should have the effect of motivating behavior and prompting decisions that improve long-term performance, and it should be assigned high priority among management processes. Instability and uncertainty, which accompany inflation and rising costs of capital, underscore the need for strategic goals for the corporation and for better ways to achieve them. Reward systems that are designed to reflect a firm's strategic goals contribute greatly to the implementation of those goals.

Some companies do an adequate job of developing strategy, managing culture, organizing, and developing other management processes, but do not achieve a well-implemented strategy because their measurement and reward system is not in tune. Successful implementation of strategy requires a very carefully designed measurement and reward system. As one executive put it: "Measure and reward managers on the appropriate management tasks, and they will behave accordingly."

SELECTED REFERENCES

Kraus, David. "Executive Pay: Ripe for Reform." *Harvard Business Review* (September/October, 1980).

Murthy, K.R.S. *Corporate Strategy and Top Executive Compensation.* Boston: Harvard Business School, 1977.

Murthy, K.R.S., and M.S. Salter. "Should CEO Pay Be Linked to Results?" *Harvard Business Review* (March/April, 1973).

Odiorne, George S. *Management by Objectives: A System of Managerial Leadership.* Belmont, Calif.: Pitman, 1965.

Rappaport, Alfred. "Executive Incentives Vs. Corporate Growth." *Harvard Business Review* (July/August, 1978).

Stonich, Paul J. "Using Rewards to Implement Strategy." *Strategic Management Journal* (January/March 1982).

Vancil, Richard F. "What Kind of Management Control Do You Need?" *Harvard Business Review* (March/April, 1973).

9 MAKING STRATEGY HAPPEN

This book reflects a holistic view of the management function. Strategy formulation is a part of strategy implementation, and vice versa. Strategy formulation, organization structure, human resources, management processes, and corporate culture must all be considered and managed together. In this way the impact of a change is seldom underestimated, particularly over the long term. Even if little or no alteration in any element appears to be required, a periodic review of the elements and the fit among them should be undertaken. Obviously, each corporation's situation is unique and, although all elements are interrelated, changes in all elements would be difficult to undertake concurrently. Therefore, the relative emphasis placed on each particular element will depend on the unique situation.

In summarizing the major sections of the book, this chapter presents a methodology for evaluating a company's strategic implementation stance: the strategic management diagnosis.

THE FRAMEWORK FOR STRATEGIC MANAGEMENT

As used throughout this book, the strategic management framework includes five interrelated variables: strategy formulation, organiza-

141

tion structure, human resources, management processes, and culture. It is shown once more as Exhibit 9-1.

The methods available and choices to be made by corporate executives in *formulating strategy* are numerous, but steps that are common to many methods include business definition, economic analysis, competitor analysis, market and company growth analysis, and resource allocation. The external focus of strategy formulation must be balanced by an evaluation of internal capabilities.

Culture involves managers' attitudes and behavior toward the firm's strategy and activities in the market. Culture is typically the most difficult element of the framework to deal with, but to ignore culture can lead to failure. Managing around the culture is usually the best course to steer in the short term. When necessary, changing a culture can be accomplished through a long and frequently costly process. It is clear, however, that a mismatch of culture and strategy will result in frustration and ineffective implementation.

Organization structure can influence the way a company implements change. Structure provides a hierarchy of authority and reporting relationships through which strategy is formulated and re-

Exhibit 9-1. Implementing Strategy: A Strategic Management Framework.

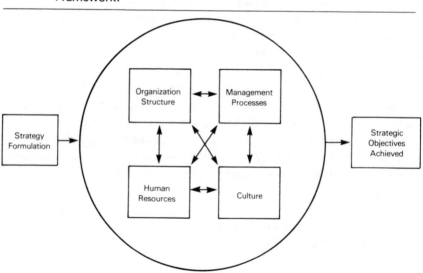

source allocation decisions are made. A change in strategy may require a corresponding change in structure. Organization structure may be viewed as a strength for, and a constraint on, the range of strategies available to a company.

Human resources is another element of the framework. When there is a change in strategic direction, major tasks must be performed for strategic change to occur, and necessary skills may not be available within the organization. Human resources—a company's inventory of employees, skills, experiences, abilities, and styles—must be evaluated and developed to meet the tasks involved in strategic change.

Management processes include planning, programming, budgeting, and reward systems. Planning enables the strategic plan to be communicated throughout the firm, and facilitates agreement and "buy-in" by the members of the organization who will implement the strategies proposed in it. Within the planning system, roles and decision-making are defined, and responsibilities are assigned. The planning system also determines how decisions are translated into strategic programs that drive strategy over a multiyear horizon.

The budgeting process translates strategic programs into an annual budget and documents other resource allocation decisions. Reward systems reflect how a company links its motivation with strategic programs and motivates managers to generate results within the framework of the corporate plan.

STRATEGIC MANAGEMENT DIAGNOSIS: A CASE STUDY

The business world is changing rapidly, and the rate of change is accelerating. Companies have been changing their strategies to keep pace with the environment. Some of these companies have not, however, created an ability to implement strategy as efficiently and in as timely a manner as possible. A strategic management diagnosis is a useful tool in evaluating a company's ability to implement strategy in a dynamic and complex business environment. The following case study illustrates how a strategic management diagnosis can be used to move a firm toward its strategic objectives:

A new CEO took control of a Fortune 500 company that focused on product innovation as a major source of growth. The company competed in a number of different marketplaces with a wide range of products, and had a reputation for growth, a high return on sales, and the ability to identify and exploit profitable market segments. The CEO was concerned about the future direction of the organization because it faced increasing competition in many of its own markets. The organization had reacted successfully to comparable competitive challenges in the past, but now prevailing business conditions had changed.

Over the years, the organization had grown complex and entered new markets. Additional investment options were available for consideration but, because of the growth of the organizational hierarchy, selection among opportunities was increasingly difficult.

The attitude within the company was that it was able to handle change. However, the CEO saw a need to review the way in which the organization formulated strategy, the processes it used to implement strategy, and the flexibility it had in dealing with rapid change. He commissioned a strategic management diagnosis to evaluate the company's ability to formulate and implement strategy.

The findings. The strategic management diagnosis showed that the company's strategy formulation process was not very well developed. Each division used its own approach. Because group and corporate reviews concentrated on operations, not strategy, division management had little incentive to emphasize strategic thinking. In addition, the top-down strategic direction was financially oriented—each division was expected to return 15% on sales and grow at 10% per year. As a result, the company had missed several strategic opportunities. Some divisions were attempting to reach return-on-sales and growth targets set by Corporate that were unrealistic based on industry growth projections.

The company was organized into about fifty divisions that had evolved over time. Division managers were given autonomy as long as they met their return-on-sales and growth targets. This decentralization encouraged a focus on financial goals, and it did not allow for synergy among operating divisions. The operating divisions were designated as strategic planning units (SPUs), although SPUs based on products or markets might have been more appropriate.

Some management processes impeded strategic management:

- The resource allocation process was decentralized. Any division that generated cash could reinvest in its own business. Cash-poor divisions, even those with growth opportunities, had difficulty getting cash to invest.
- The measurement and reward system was short-term-oriented. This year's return on sales and growth determined bonus levels. As a result, managers were not interested in long-term strategic investments.
- Human resources were influenced by a corporate culture that was operations-oriented.
- Corporate culture resisted significant changes in strategic direction.

The recommendations. To improve strategic management, major changes were defined:

- Four "Super Groups" were established. These groups encompassed divisions that were compatible on a market, product, or technology basis. The Super Group executives' roles were to manage their organizations strategically and to make resource allocation decisions.
- A strategic planning unit (SPU) was established within each Super Group as the basic unit for strategy formulation and management. These groups were based on products and markets, not derived from operating divisions.
- A methodology for strategy formulation was established, and internal and external human resources with the appropriate skills were used to help formulate the strategies.
- A new set of management processes was developed. The measurement and reward system was changed so that SPUs were measured on various bases depending upon their situations. A formal resource allocation process was established.
- A new culture was emphasized: all recommended changes would have to be taken at a controlled pace. Senior and middle management would have to be sold on any change of process to gain effective top-management commitment.

PERFORMING A STRATEGIC MANAGEMENT DIAGNOSIS

A strategic management diagnosis such as the one illustrated in the case above involves three major steps:

1.   Information Collection
2.   Analysis
3.   Feedback

Each step is discussed in more detail below.

Step 1: Information Collection

Information collection develops comprehensive information about the company's business and operations, organization, culture, human resources, and management processes from numerous sources (see Exhibit 9-2). The data are developed in a variety of ways. A re-

Exhibit 9-2. Data Requirements for Strategic Management Diagnosis.

Category	Information Required
Background Information	• Industry statistics, trends • Organization's history and performance
Corporate strategy	• Descriptions of past and current strategies • Tasks critical to achievement of the strategies • How strategy is formulated • How strategy is communicated within the organization • External environmental conditions and trends
Organization structure	• Organization charts • Existence and role of formal and informal committees, task forces
Management processes	• Existence and nature of relevant systems of planning, programming, budgeting, and rewarding
Culture	• Dominant culture • Subcultures • Management styles

view of financial statements, 10-Ks, annual reports, and articles about the industry provides an overiew of the company's major issues and opportunities. Organization charts, business strategy requirements, policies and procedures, and management reports provide specific perspectives on these issues.

Other important data are gathered from company personnel in individual and group interviews, by direct observation, and in questionnaires. Much of the data concerns perceptions, attitudes, beliefs, and values, and can be politically sensitive. The quality of data derived from personal interviews is a function of individual managers' perception of the diagnosis. While many people may prefer not to provide information, their cooperation is essential because their perspectives are at the heart of understanding the company's flexibility in adapting to change.

It is not enough to gain perspectives from inside the organization. Individuals from outside the company add useful insights. Suppliers, creditors, customers, industry experts, trade associations and, in some cases, competitors supply additional data about the firm.

Step 2: Analysis

Analysis assesses the fit and linkage of elements within the strategic management framework. The concept of linkage is important. Individual elements of the framework may be somewhat effective in isolation, yet few positive results will be achieved if they are not properly bound together.

Analysis typically focuses on achieving fit, cohesion, and some modification of existing elements. Understanding culture becomes a major factor, because people are prone to resist changes in the existing environment. It is important that a timetable for implementation be compatible with the company's ability to accept change.

In management processes, for example, these changes might include:

- Shifting the planning process toward clarifying and understanding strategic issues instead of focusing on financial results.
- Ensuring that strategic programs are well thought out, with task timetables established, major milestones indicated, and key monitoring dates set for review of progress against both scheduled activities and budgets.

- Developing budgets that will anticipate a dip in short-term earnings performance to fund increased market share, which will lead to improved long-term performance.
- Monitoring and controlling activities that will focus more on strategic variables than on financial data.
- Measuring and rewarding managers against strategic criteria instead of short-term earnings.

Step 3: Feedback

Feedback is a continuous activity during diagnosis. Its amount and quality can have a significant impact on the level of change that the diagnosis achieves. Feedback begins when a diagnostic team explains the process to senior management. Overall agreement is reached on objectives, data collection, analytical techniques, and the timetable for completion. Later feedback involves reviewing key findings developed during data-collection to give senior managers a comprehensive picture of the company. Senior management's verification and acceptance of these data permit the diagnosis to advance in the direction of future changes.

Feedback can be given individually, in group sessions, through presentations, or in reports so that senior management understands its roles within the company's diagnosis efforts and the timing of its involvement. The choice of method depends on the nature and use of the information, the culture, and the issues pertaining to the company.

DETERMINING WHEN A DIAGNOSIS IS NEEDED

Responsibility for strategic management tasks tends to be dispersed among several groups in an organization:

- Planners are typically responsible for strategy formulation and planning.
- Corporate treasurers usually have responsibility for reviewing financial progress against company financial goals and long-range financial plans of divisions.
- Human resource managers have responsibility for management development and manpower planning.

- Controllers have responsibility for developing the accounting data-base and tracking financial progress against budget and key programs.

The CEO has traditionally been responsible for integrating these functional areas and managing the growth of the company. However, as companies become more complex, the integration task becomes increasingly difficult. A strategic management diagnosis is designed to facilitate this task for the CEO by allowing for an assessment of fit and development of an action plan for the future. A self-test questionnaire designed to indicate whether such a diagnosis is necessary for a particular company is presented below.

STRATEGIC MANAGEMENT DIAGNOSIS: A SELF-TEST QUESTIONNAIRE

The following questionnaire can be used to assess a company's need for an in-depth diagnosis. Administered to key executives, the responses can be tabulated to gain a consensus on the need for diagnosis. Responses provide an evaluation of the rate of change in a business environment. They also indicate how effectively strategies are developed to meet new opportunities, how strategic elements are linked, and how the corporate culture either impedes or adapts to change.

Instructions: For each question, indicate the response that best fits the current situation in the company. Then total the numerical value of each answer and compare the score with the scale at the end of the questionnaire.

1. *How many business units (or divisions) account for the majority of the firm's sales revenue?*

   0-☐ 1 or 2 business units (or divisions).
   1-☐ 3 or 4 business units (or divisions).
   2-☐ 5 or more business units (or divisions).

2. *Does the firm's strategy formulation effort provide clear direction for the company?*

0-☐ Yes. A very clear direction.

1-☐ Somewhat. Certain data gaps exist but basic strategy has been outlined.

2-☐ No. Many data gaps exist and no clear strategy has been outlined.

3. *Does the firm's strategy formulation process consider the implementation aspects of undertaking certain strategies (e.g., changes in human resources, management processes, organization structure, etc.)?*

0-☐ Yes. We always consider the implementation aspects.

1-☐ Somewhat. Major problems are usually considered.

2-☐ No. Our strategy formulation processes focuses only on growth projections, business trends, environmental factors, etc.

4. *How would you characterize the attitude of middle-level managers toward the current strategy formulation process?*

0-☐ The process is widely supported.

1-☐ There is mixed support for its usefulness.

2-☐ The process is not considered useful by most managers.

5. *Do key middle-level managers have the opportunity to review and comment on proposed strategies prior to resource allocations among various business units within the firm?*

0-☐ Yes. It is part of our current resource allocation process.

1-☐ Sometimes. Only if a particular unit is directly affected by the decision.

2-☐ No. Middle managers are not given the chance to review proposed strategies.

6. *Does the reward system (promotions, salary adjustments, etc.) support the firm's stated strategies?*

0–☐ Yes. Performance measures are weighted differently for different business units to motivate behavior supportive of a unit's strategy.

1–☐ Somewhat.

2–☐ No. Performance measures are the same across business units and are not linked to strategy.

7. *Does the resource allocation system (budgeting and programming) ensure that resources are explicitly tied to the firm's strategies and priorities?*

0–☐ Yes. Explicitly tied.

1–☐ Somewhat tied.

2–☐ There is no linkage.

8. *Are the firm's systems (planning, budgeting, compensation, MIS, etc.) generally well regarded by their users?*

0–☐ Yes. Our staff is satisfied with current systems.

1–☐ Somewhat, although some problems are widely recognized.

2–☐ No. The systems are not well utilized and often not trusted.

9. *Are strategic programs monitored?*

0–☐ Yes. Major capital investment projects, key markets, customers, competitors, and financials are all monitored.

1–☐ Only capital investments are monitored systematically.

2–☐ There is no formal system in use.

10. *How are managers selected to match strategies?*

    0–☐ Our firm conducts systematic reviews of available staff and trains them internally or hires from the outside to fulfill strategy requirements.

    1–☐ Our firm matches human resource skills to job requirements.

    2–☐ Most jobs are filled by seniority (e.g., time and/or grade), loyalty, or on a "who you know" basis.

11. *How are managers developed to assure an adequate pool of talent in the future?*

    0–☐ We "groom" managers for future strategies and positions.

    1–☐ We conduct many "canned" management development programs (e.g., managerial skills, selling techniques, negotiating, etc.).

    2–☐ No formal or informal training of managers is undertaken.

12. *How well does the company adapt to strategic changes?*

    0–☐ Very well. Our managers are flexible and are supportive of strategic shifts when required.

    1–☐ Some resistance to change is encountered.

    2–☐ Any change encounters significant resistance within the organization.

13. *To what degree do managers expect change as a normal part of doing business?*

    0–☐ Managers expect change.

    1–☐ They expect change infrequently.

    2–☐ Managers expect the future to look just like the past.

14. *What is the prime motivating factor when the firm reorganizes?*

    0-☐ A response to major strategic decisions or growth opportunities.

    1-☐ A response to some strategic and some tactical decisions.

    2-☐ A response to tactical decisions by operating managers.

15. *How frequently do middle-level managers delegate planning?*

    0-☐ Infrequently. Managers are skilled and enthusiastic.

    1-☐ Sometimes. When subordinate staff have strong analytical and business-judgment skills.

    2-☐ Usually. Even if subordinates are not qualified.

16. *Does the planning process at the middle-management level tend to be a budgeting exercise?*

    0-☐ No. Qualitative aspects and creativity are encouraged.

    1-☐ There is financial orientation, but market considerations are sometimes included.

    2-☐ Yes. Focus on detail is usually emphasized over substance.

17. *What kind of competitive analysis is done during the strategy formulation process?*

    0-☐ Quantitative and qualitative analysis of competitor activity is undertaken by market segment.

    1-☐ Some. Usually focusing on qualitative aspects of major competitive actions.

    2-☐ Little or one.

18. *How well are roles and responsibilities defined for each of the managers?*

    0-☐ Roles and responsibilities are well defined.

    1-☐ Some confusion exists, but we're trying to resolve it.

    2-☐ Managers are confused about responsibilities, job descriptions are unclear and do not reflect actual roles.

19. *How well does the organization structure support the strategy the firm is pursuing?*

0-☐ The structure is very supportive (e.g., a divisional structure where each division's products have no marketing or manufacturing interdependencies with other divisions).

1-☐ The structure is somewhat supportive, although it can be dysfunctional at times.

2-☐ The structure is inconsistent with the strategy (e.g., a matrix organization in a setting that encourages individual performance).

20. *How do you rate the fit of the firm's strategy with its human resources, organization structure, management processes, and corporate culture?*

0-☐ The fit is good.

1-☐ The fit is adequate, but could use some improvement.

2-☐ The fit is poor, and business performance is suffering.

21. *How rigorous is the SBU's strategic analysis including value added, barrier, and segmentation analysis?*

0-☐ Very rigorous.

1-☐ Some analysis is included.

2-☐ Very little analysis of the sort described is applied.

22. *How well understood and documented is the company's culture?*

0-☐ Culture is well understood and formally documented.

1-☐ Culture is recognized but not documented.

2-☐ Culture is not well understood or discussed.

Evaluating the Results

A firm's score is calculated by totaling the numerical value of each question. To judge the need for a diagnosis, locate the firm's score on this scale:

0-17	There is no real need for a diagnosis.
18-31	Diagnosis will be helpful in managing for the future.
32-44	Diagnosis is critical in managing for the future.

STRATEGIC MANAGEMENT: IN PERSPECTIVE

Throughout this book, we have stressed that strategy formulation, organization structure, human resources, management processes, and culture all affect the chosen strategy of a company. Diagnosing their fit is the first step to implementing a strategy; making the fit appropriate for the organization will make strategy happen.

APPENDIX

COMPETITIVE ANALYSIS

Competitive analysis can benefit from an analysis of market growth/ business unit growth. Exhibits A-1 through A-4 illustrate how different competitive behavior influences competitive business unit strategy. Each circle on the exhibits represents a different SBU within a competitor's organization. The size of each circle is proportional to the sales of the SBU it represents.

The company shown in Exhibit A-1 has followed a policy of demanding a uniform level of growth for each SBU, as shown by the vertical series of circles. As a result, the SBUs in fast-growth markets (to the right of the 45-degree line) are judged successful despite loss of market share. Those in slowly growing or even declining SBUs are desperate for growth opportunities. They may be seeking out marginal customers to fulfill corporate growth objectives. For firms facing this competitor, the high-growth markets may represent opportunities to compete effectively because of the competitor's apparent willingness to surrender market share.

The company shown in Exhibit A-2 allocates resources to the SBUs with the highest current returns. As a result, those in slowly growing businesses, particularly where dominant share has resulted in an attractive relative cost position, are able to attract corporate funds and grow. Those business units in high-growth markets are not being provided funds to grow.

Exhibit A-1. Individual Business Unit Analysis: Policy—Uniform Growth Goals.

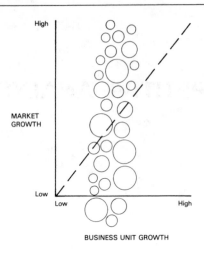

In a fast-growing business, it is easy to compete with this company where its SBUs are deprived of the funds necessary to maintain market growth. Competing with it in mature markets should be avoided.

The company illustrated in Exhibit A-3 does not seem to have any strategy. Each SBU apparently "does its own thing." Some of the

Exhibit A-2. Policy: Investment Based on Cash Generation.

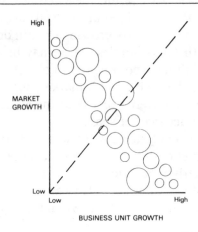

Exhibit A-3.   Policy: Laissez-Faire Investment.

Exhibit A-4 illustrates a competitor that specifically allocates resources to growth opportunities. This competitor is the most formidable. It looks at the businesses it is in. Some are business units where

high-growth busineses grow, some of them do not; some of the low-growth businesses grow, some of them do not. This firm is being managed with a holding company philosophy without taking advantage of any intercompany resource allocation opportunities.

Exhibit A-4 illustrates a competitor that specifically allocates resources to growth opportunities. This competitor is the most formidable. It looks at the businesses it is in. Some are business units where

Exhibit A-4.   Policy: Conscious Allocation of Resources to Growth Opportunities.

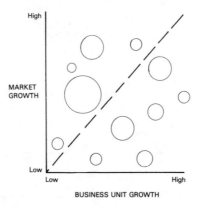

growth opportunities exist, and resources are allocated to them. These units may be in the take-off stage and might not be currently profitable; nevertheless, the units have money to invest. Other business units—the more mature—grow with the market. In some cases the units are milked to obtain cash to reallocate to the growth opportunities. Finally, some business units are seen as not viable despite their being in high-growth markets. Again a conscious decision is made to milk or sell these SBUs.

It is also important to determine the position of a company relative to its competitors. The next section describes three relative positions:

1.   The smaller competitor is gaining share in a high-growth market.
2.   The largest competitor is gaining share in a high-growth market.
3.   The smaller competitor is gaining share in a low-growth market.

High-Growth Market—Smaller Competitor Gaining Share

The growth/growth display provided in Exhibit A–5 can also be used to analyze competitive interaction. This chart shows three competitors in a market. Each circle is proportional to the sales of one competitor. Competitor *C* is rapidly gaining share from small Competitor *B* and large Competitor *A*. *C* must consider how it can avoid market

Exhibit A-5.   Competitor Analysis—I.

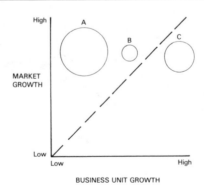

retaliation from *A*, or how to protect itself if this does occur. *C* may have examined *A*'s financial resources and other operations and concluded that *A* is either unaware of the importance of share position or unwilling to sacrifice short-term margins to protect long-term market position. Alternatively, *C* may have perceived market barriers it can erect to protect its operations. Japanese motorcycle producers growing in the U.S. market at the expense of Harley-Davidson throughout the 1960s and 1970s represent a successful *C* situation.

High-Growth Market—Largest Competitor Gaining Share

In Exhibit A-6, *C*—the largest competitor—is gaining market share from *A* and *B*, both much smaller. Both *A* and *B* must consider whether these positions are viable in the longer term. Unless there are defensible market niches for them, they will have difficulty recovering the investments required to meet the demands of a fast-growing business.

Bowmar's and Gillette's hand-held calculator businesses in the early 1970s versus the Texas Instruments dominance of this market are representative of this type of situation.

Exhibit A-6.   Competitor Analysis—II.

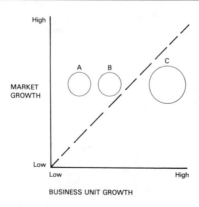

Low-Growth Market—Smaller
Competitor Gaining Share

Competitor C in Exhibit A-7 has managed to gain market share against much larger Competitor B despite slow market growth. This market share may have come at the expense of Competitor A, which is losing share. C must consider if the large investment in share gain is justified by the potential of the low-growth market. If A drops out altogether, will C's position be viable versus B? Lacking prospects for market growth and seeing its position under attack, how is A likely to respond?

Bic's attack on much larger Gillette and marginal Schick in the shaving market characterize this type of situation.

Exhibit A-7.   Competitor Analysis—III.

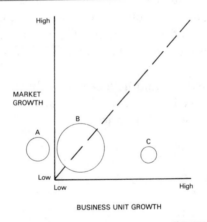

BIBLIOGRAPHY

Abell, D.F. *Defining the Business: The Starting Point of Strategic Planning.* Englewood Cliffs, N.J.: Prentice-Hall, 1980.

Abell, D.F., and J.S. Hammond. *Strategic Market Planning: Problems and Analytical Approaches.* Englewood Cliffs, N.J.: Prentice-Hall, 1979.

Andrews, Kenneth R. *The Concept of Corporate Strategy.* Rev. ed. Homewood, Ill.: Dow Jones-Irwin, 1980.

Ansoff, H. Igor. *Corporate Strategy.* New York: McGraw-Hill, 1965.

Anthony, Robert N. *Planning and Control Systems: A Framework for Analysis.* Boston: Division of Research, Graduate School of Business, Harvard University, 1965.

Anthony, Robert N., and John Dearden. *Management Control Systems.* Homewood, Ill.: Richard D. Irwin, 1980.

Banks, Robert L., and Steven C. Wheelwright. "Involving Operating Managers in Planning Process Evolution." *Sloan Management Review* (Summer 1979).

Beckhard, Richard, and Reuben T. Harris. *Organizational Transitions: Managing Complex Change.* Reading, Mass.: Addison-Wesley, 1977.

Bierman, Harold, Jr., and Seymour Smidt. *The Capital Budgeting Decision.* 5th ed. New York: Macmillan, 1980.

Burack, Elmer H., and James W. Walker. *Manpower Planning and Programming.* Boston: Allyn and Bacon, 1972.

Cannon, J.T. *Business Strategy and Policy.* New York: Harcourt, Brace & World, 1968.

Chandler, A.D., Jr. *Strategy and Structure.* Cambridge, Mass.: MIT Press, 1978.

Daltas, Arthur J., and Howard M. Schwartz. "Toward Human Resources Management." *Personnel Journal* (December 1976).

Day, George S. "Strategic Market Analysis: Top-Down or Bottom-Up?" Working Paper. Cambridge, Mass.: Marketing Science Institute, 1980.

Davis, Stanley M. "Two Models of Organization: Unity of Command Versus Balance of Power." *Sloan Management Review* (Fall 1974).

Davis, Stanley M.; Harvey F. Kolodny; and Paul R. Lawrence. "The Human Side of the Matrix." *Organizational Dynamics* (Summer 1977).

Davis, Stanley M., and Paul R. Lawrence. *Matrix.* Reading, Mass.: Addison-Wesley, 1977.

Davis, Stanley M., and Paul R. Lawrence. "The Matrix Diamond." *The Wharton Magazine* (Winter 1978).

Davis, Stanley M., and Paul R. Lawrence. "Problems of Matrix Organizations." *Harvard Business Review* (May/June, 1978).

Emshoff, James R., and Arthur Finnel. "Defining Corporate Strategy: A Case Study Using Strategic Assumptions Analysis." *Sloan Management Review* (Spring 1979).

Galbraith, Jay R. *Designing Complex Organizations.* Reading, Mass.: Addison-Wesley, 1973.

Galbraith, Jay R. "Matrix Organization Design." *Business Horizons* (February 1971).

Galbraith, Jay R. *Organizational Design.* Reading, Mass.: Addison-Wesley, 1977.

Galbraith, Jay R., and Daniel Nathanson. *Strategy Implementation: The Role of Structure and Process.* St. Paul, Minn.: West Publishing Co., 1978.

Greiner, Larry E. "Evolution and Revolution as Organizations Grow." *Harvard Business Review* (July/August 1972).

Greiner, Larry E., and Virginia E. Schein. "The Paradox of Managing a Project-Oriented Matrix: Establishing Coherence within Chaos." *Sloan Management Review* (Winter 1981).

Hamermesh, Richard G.; M.J. Anderson, Jr.; and J.E. Harris. "Strategies for Low Market Share Businesses." *Harvard Business Review* (May/June, 1978).

Hamermesh, Richard G., and Steven B. Silk. "How to Compete in Stagnant Industries." *Harvard Business Review* (September/October, 1979).

Hertz, David B. "Risk Analysis in Capital Investment." *Harvard Business Review* (January/February, 1964).

Hofer, Charles W., and D.E. Schendel, eds. *Strategic Management: A New View on Business Policy and Planning.* Boston: Little, Brown, 1979.

Kotler, Philip. *Marketing Management.* 4th ed. Englewood Cliffs, N.J.: Prentice-Hall, 1980.

Kotter, John P. *Organizational Dynamics: Diagnosis and Intervention.* Reading, Mass.: Addison-Wesley, 1978.

Kotter, John P.; Leonard A. Schlesinger; and Vijay Sathe. *Organization.* Homewood, Ill.: Richard D. Irwin, 1979.

Kraus, David. "Executive Pay: Ripe for Reform." *Harvard Business Review* (September/October, 1980).

Langer, Allen R. *The Personnel Function: Changing Objectives and Organization.* New York: The Conference Board, 1977.

Lawrence, Paul R., and Jay W. Lorsch. *Developing Organizations: Diagnosis and Action.* Reading, Mass.: Addison-Wesley, 1969.

Lawrence, Paul R., and Jay W. Lorsch. *Organization and Environment: Managing Differentiation and Integration.* Boston: Division of Research, Harvard Business School, 1967.

Lawrence, Paul R., and Jay W. Lorsch. "New Management Job: The Integrator." *Harvard Business Review* (November/December, 1967).

Lewellen, W.G. *Cost of Capital.* Belmont, Calif.: Wadsworth, 1969.

Lorange, Peter. *Corporate Planning: An Executive Viewpoint.* Englewood Cliffs, N.J.: Prentice-Hall, 1980.

Lorange, Peter. *Implementation of Strategic Planning.* Englewood Cliffs, N.J.: Prentice-Hall, 1982.

Lorange, Peter. "Divisional Planning: Setting Effective Direction." *Sloan Management Review* (Fall 1975).

Lorange, Peter, and Richard F. Vancil. "How To Design a Strategic Planning System." *Harvard Business Review* (September/October, 1976.)

Lorange, Peter, and Richard F. Vancil. *Strategic Planning Systems.* Englewood Cliffs, N.J.: Prentice-Hall, 1977.

Lorsch, Jay W., and John J. Morse. *Organizations and Their Members: A Contingency Approach.* New York: Harper & Row, 1974.

McGregor, Douglas. *The Human Side of Enterprise.* New York: McGraw-Hill, 1960.

Miner, John B., and George A. Steiner. *Management Policy and Strategy.* New York: Macmillan, 1977.

Murthy, K.R.S. *Corporate Strategy and Top Executive Compensation.* Boston: Harvard Business School, 1977.

Murthy, K.R.S., and M.S. Salter. "Should CEO Pay Be Linked to Results?" *Harvard Business Review* (March/April, 1973).

Newton, Anthony, and John Dearden. *Management Control Systems.* 4th ed. Homewood, Ill.: Richard D. Irwin, 1980.

Niblock, E.G.; W.T. Sandalls, Jr.; and J.K. Shank. "Balance 'Creativity' and 'Practicality' in Formal Planning." *Harvard Business Review* (January/February, 1973).

Nielsen, Richard P. "Toward a Method for Building Consensus during Strategic Planning." *Sloan Management Review* (Summer 1981).

Novick, David. *Current Practice in Program Budgeting.* New York: Crane, Russack, 1973.

Odiorne, George S. *Management by Objectives: A System of Managerial Leadership.* Belmont, Calif.: Pitman, 1965.

Ouchi, William G. *Theory Z.* Reading, Mass.: Addison-Wesley, 1981.

Pettigrew, Andrew M. "On Studying Organizational Cultures." *Administrative Science Quarterly* (December 1979).

Porter, Michael E. *Competitive Strategy: Techniques for Analyzing Industries and Competitors.* New York: Free Press, 1980.

Porter, Michael E. "Diagnosing the Product Portfolio." *Journal of Marketing* (April 1977).

Porter, Michael E. "How Competitive Forces Shape Strategy." *Harvard Business Review* (March/April, 1979).

Pyhrr, Peter A. "Zero-Base Budgeting." *Harvard Business Review* (November/December, 1970).

Pyhrr, Peter A. *Zero-Base Budgeting.* New York: Wiley, 1973.

Quinn, James B. "Managing Strategic Change." *Sloan Management Review* (Summer 1980).

Rappaport, Alfred. "Executive Incentives Vs. Corporate Growth." *Harvard Business Review* (July/August, 1978).

Roush, Charles R., and Ben C. Ball. "Strategic Control Systems." *Managerial Planning* (November 1980).

Rumelt, Richard P. *Strategy, Structure, and Economic Performance.* Boston: Division of Business Research, Harvard Business School, 1974.

Schein, Edgar H. *Career Dynamics: Matching Individual and Organizational Needs.* Reading, Mass.: Addison-Wesley, 1978.

Schwartz, Howard M., and Stanley M. Davis. "Matching Corporate Culture and Business Strategy," *Organizational Dynamics* (Winter 1981).

Shank, John K. "The Linkage between Planning and Budgeting Systems." In F.J. Aguilar, R.A. Howell, and R.F. Vancil, eds., *Formal Planning Systems.* Boston: Harvard Business School, 1970.

Skinner, Wickham, and W. Earl Sasser. "Managers with Impact: Versatile and Inconsistent." *Harvard Business Review* (November/December, 1977).

Spankes, John R., and Bernard Taylor, eds. *Corporate Strategy and Planning.* New York: Wiley, 1977.

Stonich, Paul J. "Budgets and Budget Preparation." In *Encyclopedia of Professional Management.* New York: McGraw-Hill, 1979.

Stonich, Paul J. "Formal Planning Pitfalls and How to Avoid Them." Parts 1 and 2. *Management Review* (June and July, 1975).

Stonich, Paul J. "How To Use Strategic Funds Programming." *Journal of Business Strategy* (Fall 1980).

Stonich, Paul J. "Using Rewards to Implement Strategy." *Strategic Management Journal* (January/March, 1981).

Stonich, Paul J. *Zero-Base Planning and Budgeting: Improved Cost Control and Resource Allocation.* Homewood, Ill.: Dow Jones-Irwin, 1977.

Stonich, Paul J. "Zero Base Planning and Budgeting—A New Approach." *Today's Manager* (May/June, 1976).

Stonich, Paul J. "Zero Base Planning and Budgeting for Utilities." *Public Utilities Fortnightly* (September 9, 1976).

Stonich, Paul J. "Zero Base Planning—A Management Tool." *Managerial Planning* (July/August, 1976).

Stonich, Paul J., and Carlos E. Zaragoza. "Strategic Funds Programming: The Missing Link in Corporate Planning." *Managerial Planning* (September/October, 1980).

Stonich, Paul J., and Robert F. Vandell. "Capital Budgeting: Theory or Results?" *Financial Executive* (August 1973).

Vancil, Richard F. "The Accuracy of Long-Range Planning." *Harvard Business Review* (September/October, 1970).

Vancil, Richard F. "Better Management of Corporate Development." *Harvard Business Review* (September/October, 1972).

Vancil, Richard F. *Decentralization: Managerial Ambiguity by Design.* Homewood, Ill.: Dow Jones-Irwin, 1979.

Vancil, Richard F. "Strategy Formulation in Complex Organizations." *Sloan Management Review* (Winter 1976).

Vancil, Richard F. "What Kind of Management Control Do You Need?" *Harvard Business Review* (March/April, 1973).

Vancil, Richard F., and Peter Lorange. "Strategic Planning in Diversified Companies." *Harvard Business Review* (January/February, 1975).

Vandell, Robert F. "Capital Budgeting: Theory or Results?" *Financial Executive* (August 1973).

Warren, E. Kirby. *Long-Range Planning: The Executive Viewpoint.* Englewood Cliffs, N.J.: Prentice-Hall, 1966.

Warren, E. Kirby; W.H. Newman; and C.E. Summer. *The Process of Management.* 3rd ed. Englewood Cliffs, N.J.: Prentice-Hall, 1972.

Watson, Thomas J. *A Business and Its Beliefs.* New York: McGraw-Hill, 1963.

Wheelwright, Steven C. "Reflecting Corporate Strategy in Manufacturing Decisions." *Business Horizons* (February 1978).

Wright, J. Patrick. *On a Clear Day You Can See General Motors.* New York: Avon, 1980.

INDEX

ABOUT THE AUTHORS

The contributors to this book are consultants with Management Analysis Center, Inc. (MAC), an international management consulting firm consisting of full-time consultants who work closely with associated professors of business and economics. The firm concentrates on implementing strategic change in complex organizations. Formulating strategic direction and programs, designing changes in organization, and establishing effective management processes—in a way that makes an appropriate strategy happen—are Management Analysis Center's focal areas. Founded in 1964, the firm now has eight office locations—five in the United States, one in Latin America, and two in Europe. Its corporate office is located in Cambridge, Massachusetts.

The book's editor, Paul J. Stonich, is the Senior Vice President of MAC's Chicago office. Articles by Mr. Stonich have been published in a broad range of business, professional, and financial journals, and he is the author of *Zero-Base Planning and Budgeting: Improved Cost-Control and Resource Allocation* (Dow Jones-Irwin, 1977).